WEST HIGHLAND
SUMMER

By the same author

A FEW MILLION BIRDS
HIGHLAND SPRING
HIGHLAND WINTER

WEST HIGHLAND SUMMER

W.R. Mitchell

ROBERT HALE & COMPANY

© W.R. Mitchell 1975

First published in Great Britain 1975

ISBN 0 7091 4978 6

Robert Hale & Company
Clerkenwell House
Clerkenwell Green
London EC1R 0HT

Composed in Great Britain by
Specialised Offset Services Ltd
and printed in Great Britain by
Lowe & Brydone (Printers) Ltd,
Thetford, Norfolk

CONTENTS

ILLUSTRATIONS

PICTURE CREDITS

The pine marten and the red-throated diver were photographed by Lea MacNally. All other photographs were taken by the author.

For
GEORGE LOGAN

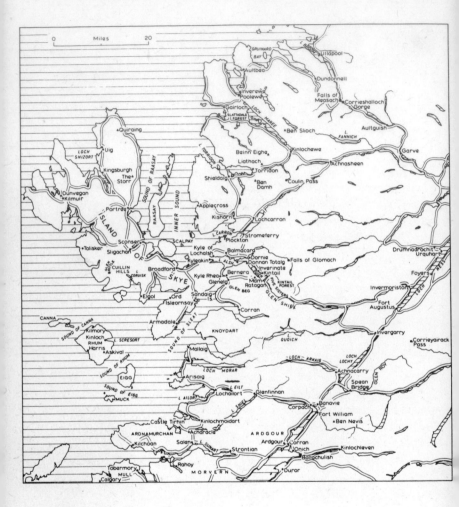

INTRODUCTION

The West Highland landscape took its cue from the weather which, generally speaking, was rather cool — and very wet.

Rain was hurled at me by a wind full of spite. Hours of teeming, tippling precipitation soaked the hills and gave every burn a baritone voice. "Och," said a native of the high rainfall belt, which begins a few miles from the coast, "but this is the West." He stode off with the words: "It's nae varra guid the morn."

The West Highlander lives in the wettest part of Europe. Over 2,000 miles of uneasy Atlantic lie between him and Labrador, which is the next considerable land mass due west of the Hebrides. People have substantial shelter from the climatic excesses. Birds and beasts stoically attune themselves to a rainfall which, in some districts, must be measured by the bucketful. I watched a red deer stag rise wearily from its hill couch and shake its body, which was momentarily obscured by fine spray.

Local people joked about the weather. I heard of a crofter who was housebound for days as rain sheeted down. His barometer showed "fair". Taking the instrument down from its hook, he carried it outdoors and held it face upwards so that it might revise its ideas!

A black-bearded Canadian holidaymaker nicknamed 'Moose' joked grimly about the weather. He had travelled to the Highlands from the dry cold north of the Arctic Circle. A common cold and chill reduced this tough character — who had muscles like steel bands and a dense growth of black hair on his chest — to a sniffling, blubbering wreck. He told me, between sneezes, "You've sure got to be tough to live in these parts!"

Scotland in the Wet!

Bens, sunk in glistening bogland, glowered at their neighbours. Some hills were indecently naked, with 90 per cent of visible rock. Burns with particles of peat in suspension ran whisky-brown. Rock faces, leaking in 1,000 places, contributed their quota to lively West Highland rivers running briefly to the sea. After torrential rain, whole watercourses — not just the waterfalls — went white with fury, for the angle of descent can be acute. One burn tumbling into Loch Maree begins at an elevation of 2,500 feet above the loch which it reaches, foaming and bubbling, in a mere two and a half miles.

Many years ago, a sage of Wester Ross forecast that summer would become as winter, and winter as summer. Events on my journey in early summer appeared to support his prophetic vision.

Yet when I began to think that the earth would never be dry again; when, indeed, even the grey seals on the offshore rocks were looking disconsolate as another storm advanced upon the coast, the sky ran out of cloud. Vapour in the glens rose like a curtain at the theatre to reveal all with clarity and colour. Then the landscape seemed to purr, and sea and loch outdid the Mediterranean in blue.

For a week or more before the sun broke through, the West Highlands had been the only part of Britain unaffected by a heat wave. Local weather was 'dreicht' (dirty). A schoolmaster, thawing out near a hotel fire after ten sodden days on the Outer Hebrides, told me that the voyage back to the mainland had been undertaken in the face of a Force 10 gale. He did not whimper. In his modest, taciturn way he was proud that he had endured without flinching the worst weather the Highlands and Islands could devise.

A member of a coach party from Inverness who shuddered on stepping into the rain at Gairloch said that as the coach journeyed westwards, from brightness into chilly gloom, she donned extra clothes and put away her sun glasses. In only a score of miles she had been conveyed from unhindered sunlight into a soppy mist in which it was just possible to detect where the landforms ended and the sky began.

On days when the sun was seen to blaze, I could admire the greens of a Highland summer. Uncounted, subtle shades of green were a balm to the eyes after a long period, through winter into an ever-late spring, when dun colours abounded. Sappy grasses, ferns and foliage, burgeoning under the alternating greys and blues of a sky that was forever restive, delighted the eyes of holidaymakers for a few weeks until the autumn decline. True summer is brief in the Highlands.

Green, in wide arcs, lay around Gairloch and Inner Loch Torridon. The breezes drew a comb through the tall grasses in the crofts, from which sheep and cattle were excluded until the end of the August haymaking. Acres of bracken formed belts of darker green on the lower hills. Bracken, a woodland plant now devoid of tree cover, took the shade for which it craved from the cloud masses. Bracken brushed the wheels of my car on the switchback of roads and tracks leading far among the hills.

Summer does not arrive overnight. Who can say just when it begins? The new season, like spring, progresses slowly, from glen to hilltop. Coastal areas, which are warmed by the North Atlantic Drift, first sense the changing conditions. Weeks later, the inner recesses of the hills respond to the warmth, which then overwhelms the high ground   that type of ground covering about two-thirds of Scotland's 19 million acres.

One day I must go to the Highlands in summer to register with greater precision the many shades of green. I recall the almost luminous green of blaeberry leaves on high ledges against dark rocks. More blaeberry formed soft cushions of green around the roots of the dark, drool pines in the relict areas of ancient forest. Pine, with its bottle-green foliage, gives a touch of old Caledonian splendour to the islets and southern shore of Loch Maree. North of this water were the oaks that succeeded greater oaks felled in the seventeenth century, when their wood, first rendered into charcoal, was used as fuel in the smelting of iron.

The Highlands were bountifully wooded until man ravaged

the landscape, which now — encouragingly — is being
reclothed with timber. The move towards re-afforestation
might have dated from the reign of James I. That monarch
planned the planting of trees extensively on the west coast.
Then James was offered the English crown; his enthusiasm for
sylviculture abated, and it was left to a few private
landowners — and later the Forestry Commission — to
create the new forests.

A modern forest of sitka spruce tends to clog rather than
adorn the landscape. We see hundreds of acres of immature
sitka, each tree of roughly the same age as its many
neighbours. Their tops are at one tedious level. Where a road
cuts through such a forest, the impression is given of motoring
endlessly down a green-sided aisle. Foresters deepen drains in
the plantations to lower the water-table, encouraging the
normally shallow-rooting spruce to go deeper. Even so, there
are freak gales that topple hundreds of acres of trees. A
hurricane in the 1960s devastated 17,000 acres of woodland in
West Scotland.

Where trees are backward in growth, phosphates are
sprayed from the air. Eventually, and before they have
attained full maturity, the plantations are clear-felled. Into
view come acres sterilised by a mat of brownish conifer
needles that will not successfully be absorbed by the ground.
The trees, being 'exotics' — brought from other lands — have
not yet the attendant forms of bacteria and fungi that will
speedily assault and break down their debris.

Scarce mammals, wildcat and pine marten, have returned
to old haunts under the cover of new forests. The big
mammals of the forest — including wild boar and wolf — are
no longer free-ranging beasts; we must be content to see them
in the wildlife parks.

The greens of a Highland summer are not fixed, like washes
on a water-colour painting. These summer greens are forever
changing. The machair — fine sward by the sea — alters its
appearance from week to week with the blossoming and
decline of wild flowers. Deciduous trees, growing farther back

from the sea, stand with arms full of leaves that become progressively darker as the weeks go by. Grasses in birch woods, banded yellow and black by daytime light, become a delicate, uniform lime-green at the edge of darkness.

By no means everything I saw was green. Gneiss hills, scoured by ice-sheets until they were as bald as coots, had not recovered from the ancient abrasion. Vegetation was limited around Torridon, where lay a plum-coloured sandstone totalling up to 8,000 feet in thickness, formed some hundreds of millions of years ago from eroded gneiss. A ruddy glow from Torridon Stone lay on the underside of cloud that hung about the area for days.

Departures from the summer theme of green included the foxy-red pelage of a roebuck pacing its territory and beginning to burn up with the fever of the rut. (The dry coughing of alarmed roe was heard during several woodland walks.) Red deer on the hill were assuming the rich red of summer, but the calves were abundantly dappled. Also exquisitely dapped were adult sika deer in high pastures near Loch Ness. With many flashes of white on their chestnut coats, the deer stood out clearly against grass that reached to the level of their hocks.

I remember the gold of golden eagles. Normally, the colour is confined to their heads, but when eagles soared in the evening, and were underlit by the declining sun, the golden effect was general. An eagle gliding by day is usually lit up from above; the form is 'black' or 'grey', terms that were actually used in an old *Statistical Account* compiled for a Highland parish.

There was bright red in the Highland colour scheme — the red of Arctic tern mandibles, briefly lost to sight as birds plunge-dived in a sea loch. Oystercatchers opened their orange-red beaks to share in a frenzy of loud piping along the tideline. Floral colour offset the monotony of green. Pink thrift blazed on the shore and yellow-blossomed iris shone by a loch. I saw white rowan flowers and pink lousewort, white clover and yellow bog asphodel. Seaside shades could be stunning when supported by green machair, tatters of golden weed and silver sand.

Bold yellow featured in the scheme. The full glory of the gorse had departed, but enough blossom remained for the shrubs to give the impression that hillsides had been peppered. The broom was flowering. Cotton grass bent under the weight of downy seed-heads. Heather, waist high in places, would look dark, rather dull, until the waning summer decked each plant with purple.

I remember the browns, and especially the moist, rich brown of peat exposed at a working near Gairloch. The 'face' of the excavation had the colour and consistency of chocolate cake. Turves of peat, reared up against each other to catch the sunshine and breezes, were marked by thousands of hairline fractures as the drying process developed.

The Western Highlands form a region of dark hill and shining water. When the Scottish mass subsided, the landscape was half-drowned. Hebridean islands were born. The sea entered glens and overwhelmed them. I had the impression of hills standing waist deep in salt water.

Into the sea lochs, between 7,000 and 9,000 years ago, early man directed his skin-boats. The first settlers sustained themselves on shellfish and anything else they could catch. And like wild mammals they thought of one day at a time. Norsemen, venturing along the coastline over 1,000 years ago, must have found in the sea lochs a resemblance to the fjords of their homelands. When land traffic was difficult and dangerous, the lochs were busy commercial lanes. Into Loch Linnhe, for instance, sailed the transports and supply ships needed to sustain the military presence at Fort William and elsewhere until, early in the eighteenth century, General Wade instituted his famous road-building programme. Straggling peninsulas, such as Ardnamurchan and Applecross, are as yet difficult to reach by road.

So extensive were the lochs that in my West Highland journey I was uncertain whether some stretches of water I approached would be fresh or salty. Viewing Morar, a

A view from the garden at Inverewe

(above) Loch Maree from Gairloch

(below) Lochan and bare hills near Gairloch

freshwater loch, on a day of torrential rain, I found it easy to accept its stated depth of 1,070 feet. Trudging across the hills I located lochans, where water gathered in the landscape's folds and pockets, offering nesting possibilities to the red-throated divers that, each evening, flew to the sea to feed.

The West Highlands more clearly matched the moods and vagaries of the weather than did Central Scotland simply because of the reflective qualities of great stretches of water. Loch Ness, one calm evening, was overspread with a delicate salmon pink hue. After an afternoon visit to Arkaig, my eyes were sore from looking at highspots of silvery light on water of deepest blue. The same effect was to be seen at Ardnamurchan Point, from which I stared across a shimmering sea to a bump on the horizon, the Devil's Cap.

One morning, when cloud cover was total, Loch Carron was a flat, gunmetal grey. The only detectable movements were of stray patches of cloud that moved in the corries as though trying to find a way out. Another memorable water mood was the turbulence of the Sound of Rhum, roughing up at the approach of a gale and being lashed by rain from inky clouds. The boat developed a curious roll. It was unkind of a fellow passenger to mention that some of the Hebridean channels were considerably deepened by glaciers; at that moment the boat may have had 500 feet of water beneath its keel!

The western sea was speckled with islands. The Hebrides contribute 550 to a Scottish total of over 750. Had the old-time statistician included the islets, such as those in Sunart and Carron on which the eiders nest? Commercial considerations loom large when islands are sold, but a notice about the impending sale of a 2,000-acre island (uninhabited by man but stated to be capable of grazing 1,000 head of sheep) also made a romantic appeal. This island held the "usual varied Hebridean flora and fauna", and had its own subspecies of mouse (but no rabbits, no rats).

Humid days in the West Highland summer are usually midge days. The midges appeared in wraiths of tawny-brown from their nurseries in bogs and patches of seaweed. Everyone prayed for strong winds to keep the insects grounded. July and August are the worst midge months. Western midges are among the largest and most voracious in Britain. "They don't just bite," said a native, "they also stick a dagger in you!" Hair lacquer was recommended as a midge-deterrent. The insects seem to thrive on midge-cream.

'Clegs', breeding on the hills up to 1,500 feet, spread a reign of terror in areas where red deer were summering, though the deer were hoping — by gaining elevation — to be overlooked. A woman said that during her first few years of residence in the Highands she went through agonies from cleg. bites; latterly it had been "nae so bad".

Mercifully, the wind blows frequently, with strength and purpose. Gales with a speed of over 60 miles an hour are relatively common on the coast. An inhabitant of a crofting township pointed with some pride to a gale-damaged cow byre, built against a cliff (the owner being spared the expense of making a back wall!). A gale forced open the door of the byre. Slates, plucked from the roof, sang through the air and one or two partly buried themselves in the ground.

Schoolchildren on the islands and mainland coast must learn about the Beaufort Scale as well as the Three Rs. Every child I met was familiar with the various wind forces. The shipping forecast was 'Top of the (West Highland) Pops'.

When I inquired about local mammals during that summer jaunt, I heard that they had "gone to the hill" to escape the heat, the flies and, doubtless, also the holidaymakers. The red deer were "on the hill". Wildcats, wild goats, sheep, cattle, all were "on the hill". To judge by local comment, summer is the time when every creature — even the family tabby cat — gains height.

In Scotland, a hill is not just a hunk of high ground. It is a spiritual thing, a sort of temple of nature. The hill is wrapped by cloud and romance. It sings to the music of the tinkling burn, which in Gaelic is rendered 'allt' (pronounced 'arlt'). Gaelic names alone indicate that there is far more to a hill than geology. I passed near the Mountain of the Rough Shielding, the Mountain of the Jumping Cow, Red Mountain and File Mountain. I heard of Lundy's Hill and Hill of the Firs.

The hill has its wild residents, among them the deer, fox, wildcat, raven, golden eagle, buzzard and golden plover. Some creatures are praised, others damned, but all are respected and are characterful in Highland folk lore. Trudging into misty corries, I flushed red stags with new antler growth (the old antlers having been cast in spring). The oldest deer would clean off (shed their coverlet of a hairy skin, called velvet) in July. I saw hinds heavy with calf, or with calves at foot. The majority of calves are dropped in June. Thin, leggy, the calves gain experience and confidence while responding to their mothers' voices and movements, and in games they play among themselves.

Stalkers were folk heroes — proud, independent, glorying in the wilderness. I heard of a stalker interviewed by a reporter from a national newspaper who mentioned his lonely life miles from the nearest habitation. The reporter cheekily inquired, "What about sex?" Said the stalker, "Ach now, wouldn't I be having a cup o' tea at that time?"

In the upper reaches of glens were outposts of Victorian civilisation — shooting lodges on the grand scale, some no longer used, standing with glassless windows and ravaged interiors. They kept an appearance of dignity even in decay. One lodge I visited had pitch-pine panelling and the ceilings were of moulded and painted zinc, closely resembling plaster. Extending from one long passage were bedrooms, presumably for staff and retainers, each room being about twelve feet by ten feet, containing a fireplace edged by green ceramic tiles. The accommodation was palatial compared with that in old Highland black-houses, which were turf-roofed. The smoke from a peat fire made an unhurried exit by way of a hole in the roof.

From the verandah of a lodge on which 'snow boards' had been placed to protect the lead-lined roof beneath, I surveyed pinewoods, a foaming burn and hills from whence at dusk came red deer questing for better grazing. The outbuildings at the lodge had decayed. Puddles lay on a formerly well-kept drive, one puddle being so deep there might have been fish in it!

In another glen, a stalker and his family were quitting the Highlands, not from choice but economic necessity. Austere possessions were being placed in a removal wagon which had a London origin. The family did not want to leave the Highlands. They had a tender nostalgia for life in the quiet glen, yet stalking alone could not provide enough money for life's bare essentials.

So, in several ways, I detected a period of change in the Highlands. The deer forest had been the pivot of rural life, and its golden age spanned perhaps eight decades. It was sustained by low taxes and an abundant cheap labour force. Shooting lodges brought architectural distinction as well as comfort for a few to the remote glens. In the formative period there was work for road-builders and bridge-builders. In due course, a considerable number of Highlanders were employed. The deer forest fashion reached a peak just before the 1914-18 War, when over 200 deer forests occupied a total acreage of 3.5 million.

It cannot have been sport alone that enticed wealthy families — aristocrats and industrial tycoons — to the Highlands for long holidays. Nor can the reason have been wholly that of fashion. The hills and glens, waterfalls and burns, deer on the hill and eagles in the sky, must have offered them refreshment of spirit.

The ordinary folk of the Western Isles had been commended to me as a happy race, with a native tongue sounding like a series of chuckles. Mainland folk also had about them that quiet, unhurried, natural courtesy to be found in remote rural areas. I sensed the old Gaelic melancholia but was also heartened at the news that the 1971 census had indicated a modest increase in the Highland population. It was the first gain to be recorded for 130 years.

What is more, the ratio of Highland unemployment to Scottish unemployment was declining.

Inevitably, someone recalled the bad old days and Dr Johnson's grumpy assertion, as the population declined, that "they make a wilderness and call it peace". Those of us who are bemused and bewildered by changes affecting the Highlands today might ponder on what Dr Johnson wrote in 1773:

There was perhaps never any change of national manners so quick, so great, and so general, as that which has operated in the Highlands by the last conquest and the subsequent laws. We came hither too late to see what we expected — a people of peculiar appearance and a system of antiquated life. The clans retain little now of their original character: their ferocity of temper is softened, their military ardour is extinguished, their dignity of independence is depressed, their contempt of government subdued, and their reverence for their chiefs abated. Of what they had before the late conquest of their country there remains only their language and their poverty.

Some crofters had faced up to the sweeping social changes. Others, cowed by unfamiliar pressures, had relapsed into a lethargy coloured by nostalgia. "Many rural problems today are those of geriatrics," a Highland priest said.

But where had all the young folk gone? The Crofters' Commission declared: "The most important need of the crofting areas at the present time is for a forceful housing policy suited to the requirements of dispersed communities and aimed at attracting young men and women back into the townships."

I heard of a shortage of skilled rural craftsmen; of young men who might have carried on the old local trades but found more lucrative jobs in new industries; of the lure of the towns and the degeneration of crofting into something of a spare-time occupation. A crofter on the verge of drawing his old-age pension hoped he would be dead and buried before the sea lochs (and he meant, in particularly, Carron) became assembly points for concrete rigs and attracted a large alien population.

Scottish nationalism can be shrilly vocal in the far western crofting country, one of the last retreats of the Gaelic-speaking Celts displaced when the Kingdom of Scotland was established. 'Whitehall' has become a dirty word. Among the Gaelic names littering the map is Cladh nan Sasunnach — 'burial place of the English'! I hasten to add that the Englishmen concerned were not murdered; they were iron smelters who died accidentally by Loch Maree in the eighteenth century.

I delight in regional differences. The West offered me chances to meet the old-style Highlander who rejoices in his independence, however poverty-stricken, and has not had his brain addled by mass media and mass thought. He is a 'character', having an individual's way of looking at the world, and also individuality of expression. Strangers expect the western folk to talk with a harsh brittleness, like hooded crows, but I found that the crofters tend to be quiet of speech.

The old folk of the West faced problems no more shattering to their way of life than events now neatly tabulated in books as 'history'. The Crofters' Act of 1886 was designed to help by offering security of tenure and other assurances after many raw deals. Yet the Act tended to fix, to fossilise, the farming pattern, which thus has not readily adapted itself to changing circumstances. Once a crofter, by intense husbandry, made a few acres yield enough to sustain his family. Today, his croft can be little more than his hobby.

Part of the Highland sadness is composed of memories of the coming of the sheep. No-one living today remembers those days, but folk memory has preserved accounts of them so tender they might have happened yesterday. Generally, in came the sheep, and out went the people, to emigrate to the New World or to huddle miserably on the coastal strip, here to make a chancy living from farming and fishing.

A crofter I met near Torridon was, surprisingly, not brooding on the past. He was more interested in current affairs, which meant the state of the weather and the auction marts. Winter had been intolerably long, even by the sea, where mildness is taken for granted. Spring came bustling in with prolonged cold and wet conditions. The red deer had stayed on lower ground so much longer than usual; it had been necessary to speed them to the hills by firing guns into the air. This man's croft was ring-fenced with high netting to prevent the deer from taking his grass and crops.

In the spring, he manured the land laboriously. The 'muck' was carted to the croft in a wheelbarrow and was heaped in a tidy pattern about the ground before being scaled by hand. The grass now grew unchecked by farmstock, but it would be August before he gathered the hay. Later still, he would lift his modest potato crop.

A few black cattle, ambling between widely-spaced conifers, were a reminder of that pastoral life sustaining the West Highlander in his grim seclusion. Cattle were summered on the hills but wintered in the glens. From these western coastal areas and the islands sprang a major part of the great droving trade in which cattle were driven on foot across a wild landscape to the trysts at Crieff, later Falkirk, and also at Carlisle; thence to the English markets.

Now the English — and their much-needed money — have come to the Highlands. Even the most devout adherent to the old ways would acknowledge the worth of the tourist industry to areas where little diversification of employment is possible. The main tourist season had not 'broken out' at the time of my visit. Most visitors, like the brown hares of the meadows, tend to stick slavishly to certain main 'runs'. Roads are jammed. Transistor sets blare. Tents spring up like multi-coloured mushrooms. There are "full" notices at the hotels and the more modest places offering only bed and breakfast, where visitors are called 'nighters'.

Stories of their antics — retailed with glee by the proprietors — are as entertaining as anything told in a native context. I heard of a couple who, surprised by the landlady as they surreptitiously fried a meal in the bedroom, thrust the primus stove under the bed to conceal it — and set the bed alight!

At a 'nighters' halt in the Great Glen, some guests were recommended to take a quiet motor run in Glen Affric. They returned to report that the glen was far from quiet; it was, in fact, "alive with Red Indians". They had seen the supporting cast of a film series based on *The Last of the Mohicans*. On another day, the Corrieyairack pass was thronged by Highlanders and Redcoats. Scottish Television had spent £60,000 in the conve sion of D.K. Broster's *The Flight of the Heron* into a children's film serial, and they were determined to have some authentic backgrounds.

Pennant, visiting Wester Ross, commented on the "kindness and hospitality" of the people. "We scarce passed a farm but the good woman, long before our approach, sallied out and stood on the road side, holding out to us a bowl of milk or whey."

It did not happen to me, but at one cottage I had fresh trout for breakfast and venison taken from a deep-freeze for dinner. "Ach," said t' e landlady, "we must think of your poor stomach. I've only been into England once. At one place they served plastic food off plastic plates. Dae ye no like fresh food down there?"

1

EAST TO WEST

I chose a long route to the Western Highlands. My jaunt began at Fowls Heugh, on the opposite coast, with a view of 'sea fowl' massing on cliff ledges high above a booming sea. I like contrasts. How better to judge the West than by first experiencing the East, and then making a single-day crossing from coast to coast?

So I went to Kincardineshire and a range of cliffs that breaks the back of the sea between Crawton and Dunottar, just south of Stonehaven. In this district I could shrug off the influence of the Lowlands, for Stonehaven is at the eastern end of the great geological fault known as the Highland Line. Everything north of that line is bound to be bigger and better!

The pastoral approach to Fowls Heugh from the main road was deceptive. I was about 100 yards from the sea before I was properly aware of its near presence. Land sights, scents and sensations dominated, until a fulmar appeared to view, gliding on narrow wings held out with an aircraft's rigidity. Moments later I was peering over a cliff. The breeze on which the fulmar rode effortlessly brought with it the musky tang of a large sea-bird community. A chorus of kittiwake cries outdid in pitch and volume all other sounds.

The fulmar returned, soundlessly, staring at me with one of its cold Arctic eyes. I saw a drab, thick-necked bird, its plumage off-white, mantled with blue. Though superficially gull-like, this was a petrel, "the nearest bird we have to an albatross in our North Atlantic waters", wrote James Fisher, who, by his intense studies of the fulmar, made the bird his own. The fulmar had the tube-nose of the petrel clan.

"Foul maa" (foul gull), cried an ancient Iceland naturalist, possibly when he had been spat upon by a bird when venturing too close to its nest. From the tubular nostrils, at times of stress, comes a twin jet of yellow oil (actually a secretion from glands in the stomach wall). The noxious fluid, which is produced by young or old fulmars, taints the clothes of human intruders to such an extent one thinks of burning the affected garments.

The fulmar, making subtle adjustments to its trim, banked and descended towards a restive sea, riding the air currents with grace as well as economy of effort. Fisher believed that in the seventeenth century there were but two colonies in the north-east Atlantic, at St Kilda and the Icelandic island of Grimsey. In 200 years the species expanded its range by over 2,000 miles, colonising the coastline of Britain, becoming one of the commonest birds of the northern seas. It is believed that the Icelandic, rather than the St Kildan, stock was responsible for the impressive spread, and that it was initially linked with the development of man's fishery interests, from which came abundant offal, food for the bird throughout the year.

The fulmar lays but one egg each year. That summer, in the West, I would see new-hatched chicks squatting on the nesting ledges. Clad in long, fine white down, fulmar chicks resemble powder puffs.

Another ringing clamour came from the kittiwake colony. Guillemots hurtled from slimy ledges to sweep low over the sea. They were not showy in appearance, being dark brown above, with black bills, but they were appealing to watch. A skin-diver, sitting on the sea bed in forty-five feet of water off the east Scottish coast, instinctively ducked as a group of these slender auks streaked near him, using their wings underwater, as do penguins. Bubbles of air trapped in the plumage gave the guillemots a silvery appearance.

The cliff-tops at Fowls Heugh were tously with gorse and grasses. The cliff-faces were the features demanding to be noticed. Here was about a mile of conglomerate — boulders set in matrixes — with ample ledges, crannies and recessions for a mighty sea-bird colony. A litter of bright shells on the cliff-top were from eggs filched, perhaps by jackdaws, from the guillemot ledges. The variability of the shell colouring was impressive. Pale blues and pale greens were lined and spattered by dark browns. Red, even black, guillemot eggs have been known, and the collectors of Victorian times prized them, swaddling them in cotton wool, gloating in private. Guillemots return again and again to specific places on the ledges. Birds laying unusually-coloured eggs thus run the risk of having them stolen each year.

The great cliffs of Fowls Heugh had a baptism of fire; they retain a strong hint, in their form and hues, of their laval origin. Having seen film of volcanic activity by the sea in Iceland, I could easily picture the formative period, with belching fire, syrupy lava and steam ascending where hot substances were being slaked by the sea. Now the choppy sea had a greenish cast; it was frilled with foam. A grey seal broke the surface, showing only its rotund head, in which the large eyes seemed to bear an expression of terrible sadness.

It was evening, and most of the cliffs lay in shade. Some rocks at the cliff-head caught light from the sun — rays of searchlight brilliance that picked out, boldy and colourfully, the mosses and lichen, thrift and campion. A stonechat, adorning the pinnacle of a gorse bush, seemed to glow from within.

When a nearby cliff-face erupted, and the air filled with a blizzard of kittiwakes moving buoyantly on the updraught, I selected a particular bird for study. The cries it contributed to the general babble were short and raucous. A medley of kittiwake calls reverberated from the faces of the cliff. The bird I kept in view looked heavy compared with the herring gulls that drifted by. The kittiwake needs to be more robust. The herring gull is a bird of home•waters, and the kittiwake ventures far from land, following the shoals of herring and mackerel, turning up — hundreds of miles from anywhere — whenever a trawler draws in a net.

The herring gulls needed ample space on which to nest. The kittiwakes shared the steepest places with the guillemots. I watched the single bird in the crowd return to the cliff, alighting on black legs that were short but sturdy. It settled on the lip of a cup of weed and mud constructed on a stubby projection. Other kittiwakes drifted in, standing around their nests, fidgetting a little, as though waiting for another excuse to tumble into the air and rouse every echo with their cries.

Fowls Heugh seems forlorn after the kittiwakes depart in autumn. Thousands of empty pouches mark the places where the birds nested. A few rock doves remain like caretakers in an otherwise dead city. When an Aberdeenshire friend visited Fowls Heugh in February he recorded a single bird. It was a herring gull.

From my cliff-top perch I heard the raucous grunting of the guillemots, which packed the ledges. Birds on eggs faced the rock rather than the sea, as though they had no head for heights. This impression, a fear of high places, would be given by the behaviour of young guillemots later in the summer when, as day faded, hundreds of adults would swim near the rocks and with growling voices call to their offspring to jump and join them on the water. The guillemot chorus of invitation would reach its peak in darkness. Birds that were scarcely fledged would respond with anxious piping calls. It might take the parents several nights of coaxing to persuade their offspring to leap from the ledges. Descending flutteringly for a flop-landing, they would locate the parents with that uncanny precision that had been shown by parents feeding young in a colony of many hundreds.

A razorbill stood in classic pose on a ledge no more than fifteen yards from where I stood. The razorbill, most debonair of the auks, is smartly black, with thin white lines indicating the trailing edges of the wings. It is said to resemble the now extinct great auk which was, however, twice its size. Razorbills were like the fulmars in that they sometimes flew above the level of the cliff-top, travelling fast and furious. Did the birds have a lingering fear that if they stopped beating their wings for an instant they would crash?

Finally, I watched the always-engaging puffin, a portly little bird that fusses around with aldermanic posturing. It would not have surprised me to have seen gold watch chains crossing its stomach! The puffin takes itself seriously, but by its postures, and particularly the appearance of its large bill — which is banded with red, yellow and blue — it looks comical, like a clown with a false nose. Puffins bring a carnival spirit to the cliffs.

A group of puffins had assembled on sloping grassland, and the mouths of several nesting burrows could be seen. Counting the burrows, or the puffins, was difficult. Birds were ceaselessly arriving or departing. I tended to pick out an individual for prolonged scrutiny. The puffin is a charmer, not least when it flies in to alight near its burrow, its red webbed feet extending as air brakes.

I could not imagine a circumstance in which I would injure or destroy a puffin. Yet Richard Kearton discovered that the St Kildans of the far west were partly sustained in their long winters by puffin flesh. Slain birds were "plucked, split open like kippers, cured, and hung up to dry on strings stretched across the cottages; and whenever a native feels hungry, he simply pulls one down from the line, flings it on the fire to grill, and forthwith has his lunch without the aid of knife, fork, plate or napkin."

From Fowl Heugh's sheer cliffs I journeyed to the Ythan estuary, thirteen miles north of Aberdeen. The coastline is low; dunes thatched with marram edge on to mudflats. Ythan is nonetheless a place for avian bustle. Hundreds of eider ducks squat impassively on large oval eggs where the dunes lie between the river and the open sea. Black ducklings, once they have dried off, are led to the inflowing tide, running the gauntlet of gulls and other predators.

Another summer sight is of young shelduck, gorgeously striped and so quick of movement that when a crêche is panicked towards the water the tiny birds appear to move on castors. Terns, in whirring hosts, call gratingly, forming a defensive ring around a thriving black-headed gullery.

When a Sandwich tern, largest of the family, flew near me, I had the impression, hearing its grating call, that its wings were creaking as the bird passed on its way to the broader estuary. Some of the rooks working a tangle of weed by the esturial waste wore white wing tags. They had fledged at the Hatton Castle rookery near Turiff, which — with over 4,000 nests — is reputedly the largest rookery in Britain.

The Ythan is famous in its own right. Here is a summer run of sea trout. During one week in early August anglers, operating from the bank or boats, hooked and landed 334 sea trout and finnock.

Northwards again, to the shattered granite cliffs known as the Bullars of Buchan. The cliff tenements of the kittiwakes did not appear to have any vacant lots. Razorbills zipped by me, and on the sea were assemblies of guillemots. Eiders bobbed like corks in a small bay. Herring gulls strode on the shore. The sea washed against rock, not mud, and its clarity could be judged from a cormorant I observed. Staring down at it from a cliff-top, I kept the bird in view even after it had dived.

The coast scenery changed again. About half way between Peterhead and Fraserburgh lay a freshwater loch, the water impounded and kept distinct from the sea by ponderous sand dunes. Strathbeg is renowned in autumn and winter for its wildfowl — thousands of grey geese, dense flocks of wigeon and mallard, and up to 600 whooper swans. My main interest was in a score of fulmars, whose frog-like croaking seemed out of place in an area where the highest and most prominent object was a headland reinforced with sandbags.

Edging my way around a boathouse, I reached a point twenty-five yards from a swimming fulmar which, without the assistance of high elevation and upsoaring air (such as it would have had on a cliff), became airborne after a frantic beating of wings. As it began to leave the water its webbed feet pattered noisily.

It was a short distance to Rattray Point, one big bulge on the coast where squadrons of migrating birds can be seen. strode energetically between dunes to a point on the beach where I had a clear view of a lighthouse. There is always bird life to be seen from Rattray, but spring or autumn — the main periods of migration — are the best seasons for viewing the traffic.

From Rattray could be seen a long, straggling procession of birds — gannets and cormorants among them. I recalled a spring day when the swallows dipped over the dunes and Arctic/common terns were moving northwards. Ringed plover scurried like mice near a freshwater stream. Twelve turnstones, in breeding dress, settled on a bank of sand, and another thirty turnstones went by. Half a dozen sand martins appeared. And around the dunes were many wheatears. At Rattray Point, with big waves booming against the sand, even the ordinary can be exciting to watch.

Westwards now, up the valley of the Dee, with telephone wires as popular perching places for yellow hammers and whinchats and a glimpse of the hoodie, northern version of the carrion crow.

It was a grey morning in South Deeside — grey sky, grey buildings, silver-grey roads, filmed with rainwater. The roadside held some fine beech hedges, then a raggle-taggle of birchland. A silver birch had attained eighty feet in height. How had a species which is so beset by fungus, and does not normally live to a ripe old age, managed such an achievement? Near Ballater stood a garron, a hill pony. I looked twice at it. A jackdaw had perched on its back.

Over to Tomintoul and the Spey, with a ring ouzel carolling from a boulder protruding from a slope in this big, dark mannish countryside. Six red hinds broke the skyline a mile and a-half away. I listened to curlew calls and the becking of red grouse. Golden plover were piping from the grassy land near the summit of the road. Wheatears flickered around rocks near the Lecht, and a cock grouse moved springily on turves newly-placed at the roadside by men engaged in improvement work.

A kindly couple invited me to have light refreshments. The room in which I was entertained was fussily Edwardian, with sporting prints on the walls and large fir cones in a brass bucket at the fireside. Such cones are plentiful in an area of extensive afforestation. I heard of crossbill invasions in autumn. Over 200 birds at a time had been seen. The crossbills favoured a local wood planted about fifty years ago. That, I gathered, was the age of tree of special attraction to the bird species with the twisted mandibles.

I was fed with scones — and gossip. "Have another scone," commanded the housewife. I refused, with thanks. "Och," said she, "I've got a box of scones in the other room." I sampled another scone and was told that Scotch pancakes were plentiful. A box of pancakes stood cheek-by-jowl with the scones!

So to Inverness, and the Great Glen that divides the Highlands. I felt a tug from the as yet unseen Isles.

The road from Inverness flirted for a while with the shore of Moray Firth and then decided to strike boldly inland as a diagonal; it became the type of road with which I would become familiar — single track, with passing places.

Such a road is frustrating in high summer, when every passing place is in demand in a special variant of the old game of musical chairs. There are rarely enough spaces for the traffic of the district. Yet a notice "single track, with passing places" betokens a real country road — narrow, winding, undulating. It feels to be part of the countryside rather than just a strip of asphalt laid across it.

Ben Wyvis became the dominating hill, its lower slopes covered by a modern spruce forest. Breaks had been left in the forest fence so that deer might descend from the open hill to sheltered ground in bad weather. These were red deer, monarchs of the high hills in the summer. Hundreds of red deer living on and around the shapely Ben Wyvis are masters at keeping away from the gaze of visitors.

Few walkers follow the easy paths up the Ben. Few strangers see midsummer snow deep in some of the corries. Though not an annual feature, it was related that Ben Wyvis was held from the Crown on condition that its owner yielded

(top) Highland red stags in early summer

(bottom) Turves of peat drying in the sun near Gairloch

(*above*) Scots pine trees near Loch Maree

(*below*) Displaced boulders at a road improvement scheme near Loch Maree

on royal demand, a snowball on any day of the year!

As a tourist resort, Strathpeffer no longer appeared to need the lure of Ben Wyvis nor the mineral springs bubbling up from shales of the Old Red Sandstone. I looked vainly for an authentic hill-walker — or even a gouty old gentleman in a bath chair.

The road led beside lochs that were grossly bloated. Luichat, Culen, Achanalt — strung along Strath Bran — were under the firm control of the hydro-electricity authority and contributed a quota to the electricity grid.

When the mouths of old lochs were plugged, water spread over intermediate land that had extended to the foothills — the sort of land visited by red deer in hard winters. Norman Nicholson, the Cumbrian poet, writing of Haweswater, mentioned the loss of the land between the old mere and the hill ranges and noted an impression of great hills standing up to their waists in cold water! The words came to mind when I beheld the drowned glen.

I cannot recall much of the journey across high ground. Mist and drizzle formed a frustrating combination. The moors were sodden, glinting with water. Burns were white with detergent-like foam. Black-headed gulls squawked and several common gulls surveyed me shyly when I stopped and walked near Loch Croma.

The afternoon calm ended with little warning of terror from on high. There was a whoosh, a clap of sound. A jet aircraft whizzed over the loch, its form rendered indistinct by vapour. The return to silence was equally swift and sudden. The aircraft's passage was difficult to recall.

A hooded crow departed. This rogue of the hills — a dark bird wearing what looked like a grey jumper — appeared equally numbed by the powerful jet plane and could not even manage a honking call. Hooded and carrion crows are now considered to be of the same species (once they were given separate status). The hoodie is a local variant of the North-west, but inter-breeding occurs where the ranges of the two meet and overlap.

Sheep farmers detest the crow. Gamekeepers are fond of stringing up corpses of hoodies on their gibbets. Egg-stealing and ripping the eyes from very young or ailing lambs are two of the crimes levelled against it. The war against crows is long and bitter.

I acknowledge that the crow has some sneaky ways, and I have found lambs that were still alive but eyeless because of its depredations. Even so, the crow has some appeal for me. It is handsome, in a rugged way. It swaggers about the countryside like a buccaneer but has considerable intelligence. And, as old Highlanders chanted, "hoodies divna pick oot hoodies' een."

Indeed, crows seem to have a morbid interest in the fate of their kind. A gamekeeper who shot a hoodie in my presence (he picked it off neatly with a rifle at sixty yards and we watched it tumble, quite dead, from an overhead wire) signalled that I should not move. Two other crows appeared; they flew round the place where lay the body of their lost associate!

If it does nothing else, the crow helps to keep the countryside sweeter than it might be by visiting carrion, tearing up and eating gobbets of rank flesh that could be breeding grounds for insects.

Mist, flowing and ebbing, gave to the hills the semblance of a stage setting for a performance of the witch scene from *Macbeth*. I sensed miles of emptiness, but not far away red deer in recline were keeping their heads low until dusk. The presence of deer was evident from the state of roadside posts, which had been rubbed. One post had been swaddled with barbed wire to discourage rubbing.

Red deer rub themselves ecstatically, calmly but with power. A stag I once watched brought a shine to a post by first working the top of its head (with its antlers extending on either side of the post) and then dealing with the space between one antler and an ear. The deer also rubbed its jaw then its neck. The treatment was clearly giving it great comfort. I felt as pleased as the deer seemed to be at its relief from irritation!

An improvement in light values was detected nearer the coast. Loch Broom lay in a watery twilight. The road dipping towards the sea was a new, good road. Even the landscape looked tidier. An ultra-neat conifer plantation was edged with larch, a species that casts its leaves for the winter and is highly regarded by foresters as a firebreak.

Summer weather brought a lustre to the coastline. A little windblown sand had drifted across the new road, however, and there was another hint of climatic savagery with the sight of conifers browned by salt spray. But the air was dry. No longer must I listen to the incessant whine of the windscreen wiper, nor the hiss of tyres against a film of water on the road. I felt slightly foolish at wearing an anorak when the people I saw were half-stripped, enjoying the sunshine.

I was now in the district where Osgood Mackenzie is remembered for his good works. Purchasing the Inverewe estate in 1862, he scanned a wind-blasted, virtually treeless peninsula and was moved to adorn it. Osgood decided to make a garden. The desert would blossom.

His success may be judged from the fact that his garden is proudly owned by the National Trust for Scotland. Over 100,000 people visit it annually. Osgood's faith in the moderating influences of the Gulf Stream was justified. I noticed an almost tropical luxuriance in a part of Inverewe which was formerly just Am Ploc Ard — 'the high lump'. First planting a shelter belt of Corsican and Scots pines, Osgood added to the noble company some birch and oak, rowan and larch, beech and Douglas fir. He also brought in scores of varieties of flowers and shrubs.

I remembered Inverewe for its contrasts. Here was lushness and colour, yet across the loch was terrain in its native state, rough and bare and rocky. With the garden and sea in such close proximity, I could watch a robin feeding on a well-maintained path bestrewn with crumbs by visitors and then glance left down to the peninsula's edge, where an eider duck floated near the patches of golden weed.

Osgood and his helpers shifted peat. Elsewhere in the

parish, peat was customarily lifted as a vital domestic fuel. Southwards from Inverewe, and a few paces from the road, lay a juicy peat hag. Turves, strewn across the ground, were crying out in the wind and sunshine. Spademarks lay as a neat pattern on the peat-face.

I crumbled a piece of peat between two fingers as I thought of the origin of this substance in long, wet periods many centuries ago. For a variety of reasons — not least climatic — organic material had not decomposed; it collected on the surface, eventually clogging the landscape. Peat lies on an estimated 1.7 million acres of the land surface of Scotland, with the greatest percentages, naturally, in the high rainfall areas of the north and west.

It is a heartening thought. With a persisting national energy crisis, every ton of that peat may eventually be needed as fuel.

2

LOCH MAREE

Two weather systems lay side by side, with Loch Maree between them. East of Maree, the weather was "cloudy with sunny periods". To the west, the cloud was heaped up so densely, and moved so little, I fancied it was collecting dust. In the Highlands it is frequently sunny on one side of a glen while the other side is rain-wrapped. Professional weather prophets need to talk vaguely!

I first viewed Loch Maree from a point between Inverewe and Gairloch, having come up from a sweltering coastline. Within a few miles I saw banks of cloud which, permanently moored to some of the eastern hills, decisively robbed them of height and majesty. Maree had about it an ethereal blue light.

Not for another twenty miles would I be able to take in the whole of the loch at a glance. Maree is indeed the largest natural loch in Scotland, the other large lochs having been tampered with by the hydro-electricity engineers.

My next full view of Maree was possible as I ascended the pass towards Achnasheen — to the summit of the main watershed between east and west. Again, Loch Maree was other-worldly, tinged by blue. The name is relatively modern. It is the anglicised form of Maruighe, an island associated with Maelrubha, who was a seventh-century saint. The loch was formerly called Ewe, hence the name Kinlochewe for the village at its head. Near Kinlochewe the rivers and burns surge into Maree and pile debris into the topmost of the loch's three main basins.

The loch overflows as a lively river, the Ewe, which after a course of only two miles is stung by salt in Loch Ewe", distinguishing it from the "salt Lochew". Punt wrote, confusingly, that "by sum it is cald Loch Mulruy". In remote times, there was possibly a single sea loch penetrating far among the hills.

My first lingering glance at Loch Maree would have been drained of its romance if at that time I had contemplated statistics. It was much later that I looked up its maximum depth, 367 feet, and was told by a man (speaking with awed tones) of excessive rainfall, such as on a March night in 1968, when six inches of rain fell in twenty-four hours.

The first vision of Loch Maree, from near Inverewe, faded. I concentrated on avoiding tourist traffic using the road southwards. My devious route — devious, that is, because Loch Maree was being avoided — climbed between rock or heather-covered hills. Here nests the golden plover (and its 'page' the dunlin). That other fine northern wader, the greenshank, is also present. All these birds can be seen in the wilds of North-west Scotland, but all are masters at concealing their nests.

Earlier in the year, I had outwitted golden plover by watching a pair for over an hour before being reasonably certain where the nest lay. I then broke cover and advanced upon it. The nest occupied a slight depression, and there were new-hatched chicks. Plover chicks are the most attractive of all the waders, the soft down appearing to have been sprinkled with pepper. It would have been unkind to the plovers to remain at their nest. The light had faded. The heavy air became almost sulphurous. When a storm broke, the plover chicks would only survive if they were quickly covered by one of the parents.

Dunlin continue to outwit me. I have never found a nest. The birds give the impression of being nonchalant and confiding. Seeking them at their favourite grounds (wild hill areas with standing water, such as peat pools), I have stalked a bird to within a few yards. The dunlin, perched on a peat ridge, has regarded me gravely, having no intention of giving away the location of a nest by an indiscreet movement, not even a blink.

Even to see a pair of dunlin at the nesting grounds is a pleasure, for this Arctic-nesting wader is in Britain at the southern end of its range. The dunlin is endearing, yet judged by human morality it would appear feckless. Research in Finland showed that the female left the nesting area when the chicks were less than a week old (some females quit even before the eggs had been fully incubated). The males left before the young could fly.

A loch not far from the road to Maree held a pair of black-throated divers. I looked out for them, having seen the pair here in spring. At that time the divers were side by side, on rain-lashed water that was as dull as pewter. One of the pair dived and surfaced with a large fish. It appeared to wrestle with the fish while attempting to turn it round.

The divers submerged together, going underwater without fuss or flurry. When they came back into view, and cruised again, their streamlined bodies were so low in the water the birds looked to be awash. Of all the divers, the blackthroat seems most unwillingly to take to the air. I have the impression that it is mechanical, for the feathers carry a high gloss and the barking flight note, "kwuk-kwuk-kwuk", sounds like clockwork in action.

A summertime gleam lay on the loch and the bare hilltops around it. Being on the sunny side of Loch Maree, I saw a landscape illuminated as though for a tattoo, the sunlight breaking through cloud like searchlight beams. The air had considerable clarity. Telegraph poles were lead-grey in hue, like a row of fire-blasted Scots pines.

Leaving open country, I followed a green aisle through Slattadale Forest. The desire to see Loch Maree was so strong I used a byroad to the shore. My car-stiff muscles relaxed during a jaunt along the forest walks. The sense of mystery hanging about the forest was dispelled when, meeting another visitor, I heard of its commercial aspect. The trees were potential fodder for the pulp mill at Fort William. Was there anyone in the district who could recall the state of the land fifty years ago, when it was open sheep ground?

Native woods, in their informality, contrast markedly with the stands of spruce. Some natural woodland was felled 250 years ago, to provide fuel for Sir George Hay's iron furnaces. The wood was first reduced to charcoal, at pitsheads, by men, with faces tanned brown like mahogany, who lived in the woods. The charcoalers had to tend the smouldering heaps around the clock, for the pitsteads must not be allowed to burst into flame. In the woods of North Lancashire, men fashioned rough cabins (which was presumably the case by Maree), and the coppice woods were clear-felled in a rotation of from fifteen to seventeen years.

The appetite of a West Highland furnace was such that each year 120 acres of woodland must be felled to keep it satisfied. The sound of the woodman's axe was dominant on the loch's shores in the seventeenth century, when twenty acres of woodland were felled every working day. Records kept at Letterewe contained a sad note: "The woods . . . were all spent up and the lease expired."

The Tollie path led me to a viewpoint high above Maree. A buzzard lumbered into the air, regaining its grace when it was able to use the uprushing wind and soar in widening circles. None of the forest mammals mentioned in a brochure was seen. Wildcats and pine martens seek flesh-food during the short summer nights. Foxes trot along the forest rides and are back in cover at first light.

Sitka spruce again hemmed me in. The species, though numbered among the 'exotics' of the British scene until a few decades ago, is now commonplace. The Forestry Commission had locally maintained an area of Scots pine, and thus showed respect for the historic species of conifer. Red deer had rubbed against some of the trees and left their mark.

The main road broke clear of Slattadale; the local tree species were now around me. Loch Maree Hotel was surrounded by groves of rhododendron. The road was particularly narrow and the traffic particularly heavy. Osgood Hanbury Mackenzie, of Gairloch, mentioned that sledge carts were seen. Two birch trees became the shafts, supported the framework and also slurred along the ground. Sledge carts were used to move peat, arable crops, manure, hay from the meadows and fish from the seashore.

Seaborne traffic was most convenient in the Western Highlands, and a sloop brought the mail to Poolewe. Mackenzie asserted that the campaign to provide good roads in the late 1840s was associated with unemployment caused by the potato blight. Surplus labour was put to work on community tasks. New roads had a high priority.

What would Osgood and his family have made of the latest road-work? Men had used bulldozers to skim off the peat and employed explosives to shatter the hard, grim rock. The new, kerbed road paid scant regard for the contours and would be adequate for two lines of traffic.

Drawing the car off the road, I beheld Loch Maree and its many wooded islets. Around me were the raw wounds of the roadworks. A considerable boulder had come to rest against a holly, bruising the tree, which was covered with dust. The air shivered to the "crump" of explosives and to the harsh slurring of machine against rock.

Long after I had forgotten precise details of the roadwork, I remembered the battered holly. The commonest of our native evergreens lives in the damp mildness of the West, but here always seems to struggle for survival; it is rarely large. Historically, it was a 'shrub layer' in oakwoods that benefited from forest clearances. The demise of the great woods by Maree gave it light and space. Prickles were its defence against browsing animals like deer, though a hungry deer will take leaves — gingerly, one at a time. Now the bulldozer was in the process of eliminating a modest holly in an area which man had already ransacked for timber.

Big John, the Post, would have rejoiced over the new road. He carried letters in a leather bag between his home at Gairloch and Dingwall when the route consisted of footpaths and deer tracks. Much earlier, St Maelrubha blazed many new ways around Loch Maree. He came here from Bangor in Ireland and founded a monastery at Applecross. He then craved for solitude in which he might pray and meditate. A Celtic saint, though gently disposed towards his fellow men, needed a stern constitution and determination. We think of him as meek and mild, yet missionary journeys were fearlessly undertaken through wild, thinly-populated regions. Wolves were among the local fauna at that time.

Thomas Pennant, visiting Isle Maree in 1772, long after the death of the saint, found that the memory of Maelrubha's good works lingered on. "The curiosity of the place is the well of the saint," noted Pennant. It was "of power unspeakable in cases of lunacy. The patient is brought to the sacred island, is made to kneel before the altar, where the attendants leave an offering in money; he is then brought to the well, and sips some of the holy water: a second offering is made; that done he is thrice dipped in the lake. The same operation is repeated every day for some weeks: and it often happens, by natural causes, the patient receives relief for which the saint receives credit."

Torridon Stone is the stuff of which the islands are made. Eilean Subhainn is itself large enough to hold a loch of considerable size. It was the fashion for those who visited the saint's well to leave a metal object, such as a coin, which was customarily attached to a tree. Queen Victoria — who loved Scottish traditions, however obscure — made an offering of a coin in the autumn of 1877. Her week's stay at the mainland hotel was commemorated by a message in Gaelic on stone and she noted the pleasure she had found in touring this part of Ross-shire.

Maree contains char, a once migratory fish that became land-locked and which survives in the depths. Brown trout live in the shallows of the loch. Salmon and sea trout move through to reach the spawning beds, some being hooked by anglers operating from boats. In September 1973, an impressive bag of 104 sea trout was lifted from Loch Maree in a single week, the catch totalling 165½ pounds. During the first week of August 1973, sixty-three sea trout were collected, the combined weight being 160½ pounds. The heaviest fish scaled six pounds.

The silky smooth road, one side of which was strung by power cables, ran near pines and birches containing typical small birds of the northern forests. Redpolls fluttered in lively fashion about the trees in more open areas. The dull, rather staid dunnock shuffled on the ground. I have known the dunnock for years as a shy, retiring garden bird. Way back in the thirteenth century, an English monk wrote a poem in which the name of this bird was given as "hei-sugge", or hay-sucker, from which hedge-sparrow was deviously derived. Such a name robs the dunnock of dignity. There are few strong points of comparison between the slim-billed dunnock of the northern forests and the horny-beaked, colonial sparrow of farms and villages.

Lifting up mine eyes to the hills, I needed a good memory to appreciate Ben Slioch (3,217 feet). Cloud lay over its head and shoulders, which was a pity. The hill's name alludes to its summit, 'slioch' being 'head of the spear', a touch of harmless fancy. The 'spear', which is composed of Torridonian Sandstone, was lost in cloud. I concentrated on the lower slopes, of Lewisian Gneiss and the gullies with their assemblages of birch and oak.

The rocks were laid down as sediments of sand and silt in a shallow sea, strata being compressed by successive deposits; earth movements shifted them about. In recent times (geologically speaking) an ice-cap overtopped even mighty Slioch. Shifting, grinding ice exploited old weaknesses in the landform, and among these was the Loch Maree fault. Water accumulated in a basin scooped out by ice.

Vegetation began to develop in this region a mere 10,000 years ago, and two early species of tree, birch and pine, are still well represented. A pinewood is a 'black wood' and by Maree is one of them — the Wood on the Grey Slopes. It has been frequently desecrated by man but tracts of forest remain which have some claims to naturalness. The trees are of varying ages, not being spaced with the grim precision of the modern conifer plantations. What remains of the Wood on the Grey Slopes is being preserved and studied by the Nature Conservancy. Trails have been opened for the benefit of the public; they led me, boundingly, between aromatic pines, and by tufts of blaeberry and cowberry, without which attendant vegetation a Highland 'black wood' would be sadly incomplete.

Our seventeenth-century observer, Timothy Punt, wandering by Loch Maree, wrote that it is "compasd about with many fair tall woods as any in all the west of Scotland, in sum parts with hollyne, in sum places with fair and beautiful fyrrs of 60, 70, 80 foot of good and serviceable timber for masts . . . . In other places ar great plentie of excellent great oakes, whair may be sawin out planks of 4 sumtyms 5 feet broad." The finest pine today is seventy feet high, eleven feet in circumference at breast height, and with an age estimated at 250 years.

The Scots pine (*Pinus sylvestris*) predominates and gives to the area a strong masculine character. The ancients called it 'Scots fir'. A distinguishing feature is the orange tint of the bark, particularly high up, where there has been some natural bark-peeling. Gilpin, a traveller in the eighteenth century, wrote of "compact bodies" of Scots pine, "the head drawn up . . . the stems becoming mere poles".

The Caledonian Forest — part of the great forest of Northern Europe — declined for a variety of reasons. In a wholly natural state, its limits or composition were not fixed. It gained ground and lost ground according to long-term phases of the climate. Forest fires, their origin based on natural circumstances, would burn for days, maybe even weeks, and desolate vast areas of country. There was the rhythmic 'shift' of the pines, with old trees dying off and new growth developing from seeds falling on the rotting trunks of the old warriors. Eventually, with a mild, wet climate, vast areas of pinewood were snuffed out by the undecayed vegetable matter known as peat. The cutters of peat were familiar with 'bog trees', exposed by man's efforts or erosion by wind and rain.

Elsewhere, Norsemen made a significant incursion into the native woodlands. They wanted open ground for sheep. It is sometimes claimed that early settlers deliberately fired forests to smoke out enemies — other men or wolves. The woods were lightly regarded for centuries. The period from Stuart times marked the destruction of pine woods for commercial purposes, leading to a debased countryside. On the Glas Leitire Nature Trail is an exposed soil section to which the Conservancy draws special attention. A layer of charcoal marks a serious blaze of about three centuries ago. The iron-smelters felled West Highland woodlands excessively. Having already desecrated large tracts of England, they shifted their operations farther north. It was the last straw.

Since 1951, however, the Nature Conservancy has managed the Wood on the Grey Slopes, and a big area around it. Natural regeneration of timber has been encouraged. Bared areas have been planted with trees grown from local seeds, collected and carefully nursed. In places, nature has been assisted, and seedlings dispersed naturally by the pines have been given better conditions for growth by drainage work and the application of nutrients. The latter has gone some way towards replacing minerals rain-leached from open ground.

Small bird life in a pinewood is notoriously hard to watch. The trunks soar with the majesty of ship's masts. (Lander noted that the Scots pine was "fit for spars", the tree being "tall, straight, of uniform diameter throughout its whole length, and free from knots".) The canopy of branches and needles was high above the ground. Small birds moved about in clusters of pine needles, and I ran the risk of acute neckache while watching them.

The diminutive siskin nests by Loch Maree, and the brighter male, of streaky yellow plumage, claims the most attention. Siskins are nesting before the Highlands have really shrugged off winter. The weather is of little concern, save that there has been a good crop of conifer seed, which is recovered from partly opened cones by mandibles working together like fine tweeezers. A fortunate walker might see the crossbill, another seed-eating bird. The bird's twisted mandibles always remind me of the bent nib of a fountain pen.

On my upward trudge, the pines gave way to birches, the 'ladies of the woods', which decked the vicinity of Loch Maree thousands of years ago, before oak and pine nudged them out. A testy roebuck bounded away after sounding the first of a serious of gruff barks. I saw a patch of foxy-red, no more, but the bark — brisk, staccato — clinched the identification. The buck was irritated or excited, not scared, or it would have 'frozen' or moved off without a sound.

Beyond the treeline lay the alpine pastures where, as dusk comes, the red deer converge to feed. Deer seem to materialise from the ground rather than arrive! With about 150 red deer in this area, signs of them were not hard to find. Red stags had lain languidly in wallows where a mixture of peat and water had the consistency of porridge. One wallow has a depth estimated at nearly twelve feet!

Dreamy days on the rocky tops are punctuated by the gutteral croaking of an Arctic-type grouse, the ptarmigan. Here is a bird for all seasons, moulting thrice each year, and in summer having a body plumage to match the season's vegetation. Disturb a ptarmigan, and it flies grudgingly, for the wings are flashingly white the year through, inviting the attention of predators.

My summer day ended. The pinewood dissolved into murky patches. Using my car as a mobile hide, I waited for a wildlife celebrity of the area, the pine marten, a shy mammal of the northern conifer belt. Local inquiries about martens had been met by a varying response. Some people remained tight-lipped. A man offered to sell me the pelt of a pine marten caught, accidentally, in a fox trap. The usual response to my inquiries was a smile, followed by an assertion that I would be wasting my time. The pine marten, I heard, was nocturnal, very shy and (though as likely to be met with here as in any part of Britain) by no means common.

One man cheerfully advised me to take advantage of a curious fact. Some pine martens live off our affluent society. "Find a litter bin", urged a villager. "Park the car near it at dusk." If I was patient and unworried by the cold and dark; if I stayed in the car and made no noise; if I switched on the headlights every quarter of an hour or so; if . . . I might see a marten. Guests at a local hotel had seen pine martens nosing round the premises, looking for discarded food.

My vigil began in half light. The summer day had refused to be hurried to its end. It reached that magical time, the 'edge o' dark' when badgers emerge from their setts. Watchers see the striped head appear. It is held upwards as the badger tests the air. Then 'our little British bear' waddles forth, first to scratch itself vigorously and ecstatically and then to lumber along the old paths, by blaeberry or bracken, to where there is food, roots, worms and the like.

Sitting near one Highland sett, controlling even my breathing for fear of alerting a badger, I heard a medley of joyous calls as cubs frolicked, two of them battling in play. During the previous hour the loudest sounds had been the three grunts and squeak of a roding woodcock passing only ten feet above my position on the tree perch; now the noise of the badgers could surely be heard in the next parish.

The sow went out of sight, to appear at the base of the tree on which I sat. I looked directly down on her. She raised her head, sucked in tainted air, and instantly commanded a retreat to the sett. Man-scent remained at the base of the tree and the sow undoubtedly got a lingering whiff of it from the hillside.

The night was for badgers, wood owls, wildcats, foxes, deer — and pine martens. I switched on the headlights. Twin beams cut cleanly through the chilly air and rested on the litter bin which seemed to glow. Insects winged into the twin beams of light, but nothing stirred at the bin.

There was a dramatic moment, half an hour later, when the light was reflected back by the lustrous eyes of a pine marten. In view briefly, indistinctly, was a dark, ferret-sized mammal — "really a tree weasel", wrote the late Richard Clapham. Then it was gone, with the sort of speed that enables it to overtake a squirrel in a tree, though a pine marten spends much time foraging on the ground for rodents and small birds.

I recalled martens, both pine and beech, I had seen in

captivity. A pine marten has a chestnut-brown pelage, with a prominent yellow throat patch; the face is keen, and the pointed ears pale at the edges. Once it was known as the 'sweet' or 'clean' mart, distinguishing it from a close relative, the polecat, which produces an especially evil-smelling odour when excited. The musky odour emanating from a pine marten is not unpleasant.

I had a nauseating tang of polecat from two animals being kept in a well-ventilated oil drum prior to being released in the wild. The smell of them brought tears to my eyes. The owner of the polecats planned to seal them in a rabbit burrow with some food, reasoning that by the time they had gorged, slept and burrowed their way out they would be accustomed to each other and, to some extent, with their new environment.

The last pine marten I had seen was in a wildlife park. A dog marten, it was about thirty inches from snout to tip of tail and weighing four and a half pounds. The marten's bushy tail accounted for about a third of its total length. It is less bushy in winter than in summer.

The marten's heyday in the Highlands was immeasurably long. It found sanctuary and food in the Caledonian Forest. When that declined, so did the marten population. The survivors clung to a few relict tracts of woodland or they adapted themselves, as did the deer, to life on the open fell. Martens took cover among rocks in the absence of trees. The red squirrel, still dependent on woodland, had a numerical decline to the point of scarcity until its numbers were augmented by introductions in the eighteenth century.

New conifer forests have encouraged the pine martens to spread down to the Great Glen and beyond. A marten was reported as seen near Fort Augustus when I stayed in that delectable place.

Yet many experienced foresters have yet to see a marten in the wild, being familiar only with marten tracks in snow or on moist ground.

The vicinity of Loch Maree, with its plentiful cover, held a stock of pine martens long after the species was extinct in

Torridon, with sheep pens in the foreground

(above) Sign marking the nature reserve of Beinn Eighe

(below) Highland cattle in thin woodland near Torridon

other Highland localities. Sir Francis Mackenzie, proprietor of Gairloch in 1835, wrote to an associate: "The keeper killed last season twenty-five Pine Martens or Marten-cats, of which twenty-four were males. "The keeper had suggested that a preponderance of males was usual. In the previous year, a neighbouring keeper slew fifteen martens, of which fourteen were males. Sir Francis noted that the death roll was "not accounted for by baits or feeding, as more than one-half were taken by terriers in rocks and cairns". A female had been trapped by a man using "rabbit-bait".

At Torridon, between 1874 and 1902, eight martens were trapped or otherwise obtained. Two martens perished in Torridon during the winter of 1863. By 1830, the population was low, E.R. Alston then believing that the species was "almost extinct, if not quite so in the Loch Maree district". A forester named MacLennan had not seen a single animal.

Much earlier, pine martens were accepted as relatively common. Osgood Hanbury Mackenzie, sage of Gairloch, recalled that his mother received an average of forty or fifty skins a year, "of which she made the most lovely sable capes and coats for her sisters and lady friends".

The keepers who trapped or otherwise secured pine martens for the Mackenzies also continued to wage the old-established war against the fox. Those who enjoyed seeing pine martens, and wished them well at a time when they faced extinction, did not entertain serious doubts about the fox's ability to survive. One might just as well try to exterminate the rabbit!

I have already confessed to admiring the hooded crow. (I dare not admit it to my friends on the sheep ranges of Lakeland and the Pennines). I also admire some of the characteristics of the hill fox, not least its ability to survive by craft and cunning.

In the Highlands, a crofter told me of springtimes when, with the vixens hunting for food to deliver to their cubs, a shepherd might lose thirty or forty of his lambs. Traps were set for the fox. Stalkers with dogs would locate a fox earth in spring and set the terriers to the grisly task of destroying the cubs. Then the men would organise a round-the-clock watch for the return of the vixen. It might be two or three days before the vixen's curiosity got the better of her and she came in to investigate the earth. Such a fox was in a dilemma. Its fine senses would inform it that man was present, yet the mother love would decree it must investigate.

The final approach of the fox to its ravaged earth was usually under cover of darkness. A watcher would see the silhouette of the fox on the near skyline. Switching on a spotlight, he would confront the nervous animal and raise his gun to destroy it.

A hill fox lies up in a borran, cairn or other rocky place up to 2,000 feet above sea level. Summer daytimes may otherwise be spent in dozing on some blaeberry-covered ledge. The hunting trip begins with the coming of night. Highland foxes tend to be truly wild, to avoid the haunts of man, and so hens and chickens are not often taken. In open country, shepherds or gamekeepers can track them down and destroy them, but man is nearly helpless when big conifer forests are planted. Setting traps for foxes is doubtless an expression of frustration.

Alas, not only foxes put their foot in traps. There are times when a man going the rounds finds, instead, the carcase of a shy — and scarce — pine marten.

3

THE OLDEST GLEN

The road from Kinlochewe to Torridon lay down what has been called the oldest glen in the world. The 'oldest glen' was sinister — murky, misty and still. A wheatear, flickering and chacking, seemed anxious to re-animate the dull, cloud-beset scene. It was a cock bird, the size of a robin but wearing a jacket of French grey. The bird's white rump, from which it is named, looked the brightest feature of the glen.

Before I left the sunlit areas near Loch Maree; before the light went flat (my spirits shortly followed), I had surveyed the glowing tops of the Beinn Eighe group of hills. Mist sneaked furtively into a corrie so big that the mountain seemed to be yawning. Backlit by the sun, the vapour was as light in tone as were the screes of Cambrian quartzite that characterise Beinn Eighe and from which it is named 'Mountain of Ice'.

This 3,309-foot hill calls for respect. If I had worn a cap I should have doffed it. An admirer exulted:

> Benyea, magnificent Alp,
> Blanched bare and bald and white;
> His forehead like old sea-eagle's scalp
> Seen athwart the sunset's light.

The name of the Beinn Eighe nature reserve was cut on a horizontal piece of wood supported by rough stonework. Some young conifers sat up prettily not far away, but the general impression was of open landscape, austere, sodden. In antiquity, the oldest glen in the world was filled with timber. Locals asserted that a squirrel might pass from one tree to another, without touching the ground, all the way from Kinlochewe to the sea.

The rocks, not the glen, are immeasurably old. Ice sheets

cleaned up the area a few thousand years ago. They over-rode it, gouged and plucked at it, removed the debris of the years and gave it smooth and sweeping forms. Torridonian Sandstone lay around me. Normally the rock that is named after this region has an ember-like tone, but my thoughts about fire were short-lived. Water poured from the hills as though they were sponges. The terraces and slopes concealed by the mist there, might have held a thousand more runnels.

Local features had a dark grandeur. I saw typical 'greeenshank country' — bog, pine and lochan. A raven croaked. Sacred to the Norseman, this bird was high on the list of vermin during the Victorian sporting period. Even today some gamekeepers get an itch in their trigger finger when they see its dark form flying near the crags.

Few tourists stirred on the winding road down the glen. Tourists, like bees, tend to count only the sunny hours. Early in the day, the local golden eagles soar over the remnants of the old forest, seeking food and usually finding it soon enough to be able to spend most of the daytime at some lofty perch, seeing but unseen. Black-throated divers rear young on larger stretches of water. Red deer are less common in this craggy district, where good grazing is limited, than where the landscape has fewer outcropping rocks.

Where were the native people? The Forest of Coulin and around Loch Clair were populated in summer even before tourism developed. Here were the huge hill grazings for the stock of the folk of Kinlochewe. The home acres at the township were thus given a respite from grazing until harvest-time. Mackenzie of Gairloch explained that before the crofters' arable land was turned into four-acre crofts; before the 'runrig' (a communal system) was abolished in favour of individual holdings, each family went with its cattle to a shieling for two or three of the summer months. "When the great change was made, one of the new ideas for the betterment of the smaller tenants was that they should give up their migrations to the shieling, and consume the grass of their distant hill pastures by grazing them with sheep, instead of with cattle."

Standing in a misty stillness, I tried to picture life as it was on the summer hills. Cattle were of prime importance, not as food for the peasant who reared them but (through their sale) as payment for rent. Cattle helped the rearer to make some ready cash for the few items that must be purchased. Black cattle — the colour associated with hardiness — were almost as common as are sheep today.

I thought of the simple shielings and the folk who looked after the cattle, making cheese or butter from the milk. The writings of Carmichael helped, though he was not writing about Torridon. "Having finished their tillage," he explained in 1880, "the people go early in June to the hill grazings with their flocks. This is a busy day in the Townships. Like bees about to swarm, the families bring their herds together and drive them away. The few sheep lead, the cattle next, and horses follow."

Men had loads of sticks, heather ropes and spades, for the summer huts or shielings must first be repaired. "The women carry bedding, meal, dairy and cooking utensils. Round below their waists is a thick woollen cord or leather strap, underneath which their skirts are drawn up to enable them to walk easily over the moors. Barefooted, bareheaded boys and girls with dogs flit hither and thither, keeping the herds together, and now and then having a neck and neck race with some perverse animal that tries to get away."

It was a noisy migration. "Men several at a time direct and scold. Women knit, sing, talk and walk as free and erect as if there were no burdens on their backs nor in their hearts. Above this din, sheep bleat, cows low and mares neigh. All who meet them on the way bless the trial, as it is called, and wish it a good flitting day.

"When the shieling has been reached and burdens laid down, the huts are repaired, fires kindled and food prepared. The people bring forward every man's stock separately, and as they are driven into an enclosure the constable and one other on either side of the gate see that only the proper souming has been brought. Then the cattle are turned out to graze." A simple feast followed. "They say grace, and every head is uncovered and every knee bowed, as they dedicate themselves and their flocks to Christ . . ."

Carmichael describes the accommodation: "The walls of shieling huts are of turf, the roofs of sticks covered with divots. Usually two huts are together, the larger being the dwelling, the smaller the dairy."

Mackenzie noted that people going to the shielings took with them their sheep and goats. "These had to be carefully herded by the children all day, to keep the lambs and kids from being carried off by eagles and foxes. At night at the shielings, the sheep and the goats were driven into bothies and bedded with bracken or moss, and when these bothies were cleaned out in the spring they contained a large accumulation of excellent manure for the potatoes." The cattle were driven south to be sold at the trysts.

Living on the hills in summer, and returning to the home farm for the winter, was a Norse idea on my native Pennines. Their word 'saetr' became incorporated in many dalehead place-names. The foundations of huts seen during Highland hill walks spoke to me (but not clearly enough!) of summer days long ago. Cleansing winds long since removed other traces of the shieling way of life.

Do those winds still carry, occasionally, the whiff of peat fire from a whisky still? Here was another hillside occupation. It was quite illegal. A distillery was established in Coulin forest. The Revenue men of that time were wise to the ways of the distillers, and their noses were well-educated to the distinctive tang. How would the more innocent Revenue man fare today if he went looking for an improvised distillery on the wild wastes above the oldest glen? Those who drank some of the liquor had a sensation akin to a rough file being thrust down their throats!

Ian Macdonald, in *Smuggling in the Highlands*, related that a still was discovered near the foot of Bein Alligan. Another had been established at the edge of a loch, and a new copper was found buried in the moss on an islet. In the nineteenth century "everybody, with a few exceptions, drank what was in reality illicit whisky, which was far superior to that made under the eyes of Excise".

Highland distilling may have been crude, but the operation was basically sophisticated. The starch of the barley grain was softened by being placed in and steeped in a burn. The grain was then spread for germination in some remote cave or in the loft of a building far from the road. The drying kiln was stoked up with peat, and peat fire came into its own again for the protracted 'mashing'. The still had a 'worm', a curious name for the coiled copper piping in which hot vapour condensed into liquid. Camouflaging a still called for endless ingenuity. One man built his still-house near a waterfall so that the emanating smoke would blend visually with spray from the tumbling water!

I moved out of the oldest glen. Torridon came into view. The sky lightened by several shades, for the sea was near. Torridon's main concentration of buildings stood like a string of white beads alongside Liathach (3,456 feet.) Newly-shorn Cheviots and their lambs wandered along the main road and grazed its verges. Liathach rose sheerly beyond the houses, and it terrified me to look at the hill because the screes looked unstable. Although 1,000 tons of boulders were poised over every dwelling, yet none of the local people I saw had a nervous twitch. None gave the impression of having missed a night's sleep through worry.

This was crofting country. The Crofters' Act of 1886 defined a crofter as "a small tenant who finds in the cultivation and produce of his croft a material portion of his earnings and sustenance". I attempted to compare the ideal with reality. The Act was popular when introduced because crofters then had security of tenure; they were able to own their homes, while paying rent to the laird for the use of land, including that on which the homes stood. Buying and selling of crofts among themselves was not allowed; so the croft remained small.

Crofting laws confuse a stranger. I was amused to read an

advertisement in a magazine for a croft which stated that "the transfer of crofts is subject to stringent conditions. If you are not aware of them you are probably not eligible anyway!"

I had a fellow-feeling with the crofters. Small-time farmers on the Pennines, whom I have known for many years, have faced similar problems connected with viability. Crofters are not peasants, existing in primitive conditions. Like smalltime farmers the country over, they are proud of their calling, and also of their independence. Crofts are small-holdings of from five to ten acres. Where, as often happened, they were grouped together in 'crofting townships', the crofters have shared grazing rights on common pastures.

Now each crofter seems to feel himself very much on his own. One sadly contrasted the present situation with the time when mutual help was common with shearing the sheep, harvesting the crops, cutting and carrying peats, even (in coastal townships) with the construction of boats and the fishing itself. Farmers in Northern England frequently came together in a demonstration of mutual help. At sheep-clipping time on Cumbrian farms, for instance, several families worked on the same flock, then moved on to the next; they co-operated until the massive task was completed on a district basis.

To read of the old crofting days, when the work was labour-intensive, is to marvel at what men and their families could achieve with limited implements. There was at least an abundance of labour. The heartfelt prayer of the over-worked, under-remunerated Scottish crofter was:

> O that the peats would cut themselves,
> The fish jump on the shore,
> And that we all in bed might lie
> For aye and evermore.

A crofter's land near Torridon resembled an open prison, so tall was the fencing reared around it to keep out sheep and red deer. The sheep had grazed the land until the lambs were strong, and then the crofter spread farmyard muck and left the croft to itself. The summer flush of grass would be mown — by hand — and become hay. The sheep are assembled in due course for the clipping, which provides a free entertainment for visitors. "You can hardly see the sheep for people", said the crofter. "Cameras are clicking away hour after hour. I suppose they've got to spend their money on something!"

Wooden pens near the shore received the sheep for clipping and other routine tasks like dipping. The hoggs are clipped in June, and the ewes lose their jackets in July. Black-faced sheep and Cheviots populate the district, and the blackface (I was told) has a fleece weighing from five to six pounds, depending on the quality and condition of the animal, which depends on the weather of the immediate past, which depends . . .

The blackface is a well-tried breed and, with the Welsh Mountain, has the distinction of being the most popular in Britain. Each claims over a million ewes. Torridon sheep, the blackface especially, need to have strong and steady legs; they roam craggy hills to elevations above 3,000 feet. At gathering time "ye canna use a dog till ye've reached some level grund. Or the sheep'd panic and tummel from the crags."

The crofter told me of a summertime pest, the tick, which is harboured by dense bracken. Foxes take young lambs, but the crofter was not allowed to trap foxes. He lamented: "Everything's protected now." A wise shepherd could tell instantly whether a lamb had been attacked by a fox or an eagle. A fox bit off the tail of a lamb, and then tended to divide the rest into two, taking half away and, perhaps, returning for the rest. An eagle took a lamb, and stripped the wool from it, 'dressing' the corpse for delivery to the eyrie.

Haytime is the main preoccupation in summer. There must be a great deal of fodder to sustain farm animals during the winter, which, though milder here than in Central Scotland, can have a sting in its tail. On the hill holdings, the men like to see half the fodder remaining in mid-February. The crofter would mow the grass with a scythe, sharpening the blade with a carborundum stone. A keen edge to the blade ensures that the swathes are long and neat. I have chatted with Pennine farmers who remembered when teams of men with long-bladed scythes moved across the meadows. Today, in England, the machines are in command. The crofter knew the term 'strickle' for a piece of wood attached to the scythe. It was removed when the blade had to be sharpened. Strickles used in the Highlands were plated with a carborundum material, I heard. On the Pennines, the strickle was pitted with holes, smeared with bacon fat and dusted with a fine hard sand of the type that could be collected from hill tarns. The sand worked its way into the holes, was held there by the fat, and provided an excellent abrasive surface.

From the croft, came a rasping sound, that was not produced by a ghost using a strickle. We listened to the voice of the corncrake which, once heard widely by night as well as day, has become uncommon in many parts of Britain.

Torridon may change with the passing years, but it will not decay. In May 1967, the Torridon estate of 14,100 acres passed into the ownership of the National Trust for Scotland, which then added to it, from a gift, the 2,000-acre estate of Alligin Shuas. The warden, Lea MacNally, was a stalker on Ness-side before he moved to Torridon. Lea now has a national reputation as a naturalist, having written books about Highland wild life, illustrating them with superb photographs. His small deer museum contained deer heads, pictures, specimens of parasites, and much else.

Roe deer flit, insubstantial as shadows, through woods by upper Loch Torridon. Other roe live out on the hills, couched on rank heather. A roe doe has its fawns at foot during benevolent summer. The birth-time is May or early June, and towards the end of July and into August comes the rut, when bucks pursue the coquettish does and mating occurs. Because the implantation of the embryo in the doe's womb is delayed until December, fawns are born when the weather and availability of food are best suited to their survival. The roe, being small and compact, has needed to change little since prehistoric times. Other species of deer are socially-minded, but the roe tends to be a loner or to live in small family groups.

From Torridon I followed one of the improved roads up the hill and across to Shieldaig, with a halt to scan Upper Loch Torridon, together with its arc of lush grass, the string of white houses and great hills bonneted with cloud. At Shieldaig I saw eider ducks with half grown young. The first of the year's infants had been seen on 5th June. A 'lazy' tide, calm as a park lake, lapped half-heartedly against mud, sand and weed. An oystercatcher probed for food, and a cormorant stood hunched, with unfurled wings, like a Germanic emblem. The heron that stalked the shallows was perfectly reflected in the water; I looked obliquely down on the bird from the roadside, maybe fifty feet above sea level. The bird moved with hunched body, neck low, yellow beak poised to strike.

The hinterland to which I returned was gloomy. A mist of such liquid consistency it verged on drizzle took the hard, clean lines from another majestic remnant of the Caledonian Forest. Pines of various ages extend up a ledged hillside. Once the forest extended far from Glen Shieldaig, and Wilson (1842) was informed by the local fishery officer that in his early days – about fifty years previously – "the whole surrounding country to the south . . . was covered by a forest of firs of great magnitude".

A sandpiper scurried along the road, not far from the river. A camper had pitched his tent near an electricity pole, to which he attached one of the main guy ropes.

A picture postcard farmstead stood long and low, bright with white paint, beside a wooded gorge in which I could see tumbling water. In front of the farmhouse lay a shallow, reed-edged loch. Fields round about contained shorn Cheviots.

In mist so thick I could taste it, I decided not to renew an acquaintanceship with the Pass of the Cattle to Applecross. The name of this peninsula is more appropriate to a southern vale than a rocky arm of the Scottish coast. "Applecross", boomed the *Statistical Account* of 1794, "is a fanciful designation assumed by one of the proprietors of that part of the parish . . . The ancient and only name by which it is known in Gaelic is Comrich, signifying protection . . . ."

The road to Applecross starts innocuously; then the Pass of the Cattle (Bealach nam Bo) zig-zags daringly over the hill, rising from sea level to 2,054 feet in six miles. Road-makers are improving a route from Shieldaig to Applecross. Meanwhile, the pass is the only approach for wheeled traffic. It lies between the redstone hills of Meallgorm (2,325 feet) and Shurr a Chaeorachain (2,600 feet). Bends are sharp, but less acute than they were. A local man told me, "They're nae so bad now. I ken when you had to reverse a wee bit to get round the worst of them."

The climb is doubly memorable if you have good visibility at the summit, and gaze across to Skye and the Outer Hebrides. Trust a saint to find such an out-of-the-way place! Here ministered St Maelrubha (already noted under Loch Maree). He doubtless made his approach to Applecross by boat, as do many people today.

Historical record and folk memory keep alive the doings of St Maelrubha. People sacrificed bulls on his day, 27th August, and the custom was denounced in the seventeenth century as an "abominable and heathenish practice". Locals believed that this was the way by which sick people would have their health restored; quite how is not explained.

Was there not an echo here of Pictish times, when bulls were sacrificed as a form of diversion? The custom could have been a survival of a faith older than that brought by Maelrubha and his missionaries.

4

INDOMITABLE EIDER

The eider — a big, blunt, tough-looking sea duck — came into view at many points along the west coast. Seeing it keep perfect station a yard or two from where rocks were being smothered by spray I had the impression it was riding at anchor. Eiders also bobbed on salt-water lochs far from the open sea.

When I disturbed an eider during its afternoon reverie on land, I noticed its erect walk to the sea, though it had a slow, rolling gait — the sort that marked out sailors from landsmen. Another eider, taking flight in calm weather, pattered its feet on the sea before lifting itself aloft. A group of eiders seemed to prefer a follow-my-leader formation when in flight. So close were they to the water they could have looked down on their reflections.

The crooning of eider, a haunting sound like that made by the grey seals, was not often heard now that summer had arrived. Everywhere, matrons swam with the year's young, and so close did the smallest ducklings stay to the adults they might have been attached to them by towlines. Tiny, down-covered youngsters moved confidently, with great surges of power, in the roughest water. At other times I saw them in recline on rocks, soaking up the summer sunshine.

Finding a bleached log near the head of Loch Carron one evening, I sat down to watch the eider moving on a high tide. Ducks and ducklings had great assistance from the inflowing sea. The large, robust eider duck (they can weigh over four pounds), was a Plain Jane, wearing a dull-brown plumage that was mottled and barred by brownish-black. That day all the fine detail of the plumage was lost as birds swam under low cloud and against the tidal greys.

An eider is plain in shape — thick-set, with a large triangular head. This effect is produced by the continuation of the forehead directly along the slate-grey beak. A short neck connects the head to a full, roundish body that is as featureless as a curling stone. An eider looks waterlogged because it swims with its tail against the water, not held up.

New-hatched ducklings are swaddled in a darker shade of brown than that of adult females. The ducklings breasting Loch Carron, as high tide smacked its lips against the marsh, stayed close to the females in the best traditions of the convoy system. The common enemy was the large gull, notably the great black-backed gull, which enjoys flesh-food at mealtimes.

When a duckling swam hard, I marvelled at the power being generated by the diminutive webbed feet. At times, it seemed to want to run on the waves. It moved wherever it wished, being gloriously independent of the boiling and frothing tide. Was the nearest female its mother? Or another bird, even an unsuccessful breeder, happy to find an outlet for its strongly-developed maternal instincts? Creches are formed on the summer sea, with a few adults in supervision. The creche habit has been developed by the shelduck, another marine species.

The eider was apparently confined to the isles until the middle of the nineteenth century. A visitor to Sule Skerry commented on the presence here of the big sea ducks as long ago as 1582. As the eider population increased, surplus birds would come to the mainland, and from thence they spread to every suitable stretch of the Scottish coast, even (as I had seen north of Aberdeen) facing the brisk tides of the east coast.

Eiders have been steadily expanding their range on other North European coasts. My first serious studies of the bird were undertaken as far south as Walney Island, near the shipyards of Barrow-in-Furness. Nesting began here as recently as 1949 and now there are about 400 pairs, with flocks of up to 1,000 in winter.

Eider have made the Scottish coast their own. As summer progresses, and the ducklings gain in size and strength, birds that nested around the head of Carron are seen lower down the loch. Visitors to the village who look from bedroom windows at the boarding houses in the early morning see eiders disporting themselves close to the shore.

The eider is so large it cannot be overlooked when on the sea. The drake is especially prominent when in its nuptial finery of bold pied plumage. Eiders assemble in strength where there are substantial beds of mussels, for which they dive or sometimes even dabble. Either their beaks are unduly strong or they have developed the knack of easily opening mussels. It is no mean feat. The bird's digestive juices must be well concentrated to tackle the tough marine fare.

On the Northumbrian coast, the eider is known as Cuddy's Duck after Cuthbert, a Scottish saint summoned to be a missionary in barbaric Northumbria. Later in life, the meditative Cuthbert was fond of leading a solitary life in remote places, such as the Inner Farne, where eider nested. In protecting the eider and other sea birds, St Cuthbert became a pioneer British conservationist.

The notion that the eider was spared persecution because of the interest the saint showed in it may be nothing more than medieval romance. Northumbrians do tend to leave it alone, and it swims confidingly in Seahouses harbour, from which boats sail to the Farne Islands. A local fisherman said the eiders were left in peace because their flesh is unpalatable. Only a starving man, marooned on one of the islands without immediate hope of food, would consider eating it!

In the Hebridean context, the eider has not been persecuted. Gavin Maxwell, who wrote the classic *Ring of Bright Water* at his cottage retreat on the mainland overlooking Skye, actually had a notion to 'farm' the eider on one of the islands. In return for providing it with secure nesting facilities, he would collect and market the down with which the ducks would lag their nests. Icelanders had been doing this for 1,000 years. Viking settlers improved the harvest of down by encouraging the birds to use prefabricated stone shelters.

Eider farming can be profitable. The species is colonial in

suitable places, and one colony in Greenland holds an estimated 10,000 nests. It has been found that the bird derives pleasure if coloured ribbons, or instruments making sweet sounds when activated by the wind, are set up on the breeding grounds.

As for me, eiderdown is much over-rated as a bedding material. When, occasionally, I have slept on a down-filled mattress I have had an impression of being suffocated or of being suspended in space. My grandmother had an 'eiderdown' of which she was greatly proud until a seam split, some fine feathers appeared to view and they were identified as coming from domestic ducks!

Behold the drake eider as it breasts a flow tide in May. Birds are then beginning to disperse in pairs, and feelings among rival males can run high. The duck still looks drab (it must not be conspicuous when incubating eggs), but the drake is brilliant. Though dominantly black and white, there is a tinting of pale green on the sides of the white head and the nape, and delicate pink suffuses the white of the upper breast. Black feathers cover the crown, flanks, belly and tail.

An eider drake is thus one of the most prominent of the wildfowl, revealing itself dazzlingly to the gaze of the world. In the courtship display comparatively little subtlety is shown. The head is jerked upwards, and a crooning sound — "ah-oo, ah-hee-oo" — can be heard.

A Victorian moralist would not have found pleasure in thinking about the eider. Hearing about its life, he would accuse the drake of having no sense of responsibilities; of mating and then clearing off, to enjoy itself before going into the moult. Modern studies have shown that the male helps to select a nest site and, indeed, may sit beside the female at night for a short period before leaving the area. If the drake remained near the nest it would draw unwelcome attention to it, the female, on the other hand, being concealed by a cryptic pattern.

The eider duck sits patiently, tranquillized by hormones, rarely if ever leaving the simple scrape of a nest which is lined with pieces of vegetation and then becomes lagged with the

(above) Pine marten

(below left) A herring gull takes flight *(below right)* A roe doe

(top) Cheviot sheep on the marshes by a western sea loch

(bottom) Ardaneaskan, near the mouth of Loch Carron

greyish-brown down that the female has plucked from its breast (a custom among other ducks, also swans and geese, and by no means restricted to eiders). Incubation begins when the clutch of large, oval, greenish eggs is complete. Eventually, the down becomes tangled with debris and vegetation, but there is so much of it that it spills across the rim of the nest.

The first of the year's young go to the sea in June. Some broods are led away by the female soon after hatching. Or she may restrain the ducklings, awaiting the most favourable combination of weather and tide. Many ducklings must be taken down to the sea at night. The surreptitious approach is necessary if the young are to escape the attention of predators. I have watched herring gulls sweeping down on an eider duck that squatted on the beach, the ducklings beneath her.

In late June or early July, the showy drake is in 'eclipse'. The bright and bold plumage of the spring is exchanged for one that is dingy black.

My last view of the eiders of Loch Carron was from the village of Ardaneaskan, near the 'jaws' of the loch. Eider nest on some of the islands, here and off Kishorn. The great black-backed gulls are in attendance. A duck's brood of eight ducklings may have become five, then three, on successive days. Such predation does not seriously imperil the eider population. A local man told me there were between 500 and 800 eiders in the locality, and some immense rafts were to be seen in winter.

At Ardaneaskan, the nearest eider was a duck at its toilet. As I watched, spray flew as the bird beat its wings against the sea. The eider bent and twisted its head, using its beak to groom the feathers of its tail. Beating its wings again against the water, it rose up to beat them in the air, and then tucked them neatly away.

The eider cruised serenely away — a Plain Jane, its dark feathers made doubly plain by being clearly reflected in the water.

5

AROUND LOCH CARRON

Every hill beside Loch Carron was tabular — neat, but lacking in splendour. Carron's splendid skylines were obscured by cloud which looked dense enough to form a roosting place for gulls.

Cloud reduced the hills to a tediously uniform height, and the lightest part of the scene was the loch itself. The evening had also "set in with rain", a phrase I plucked from Robert Southey's account of his Scottish tour in 1819. Rain, he added wearily, was a circumstance to be expected in this region. Southey, advancing towards the west, did find that "the blackness of the hills" gradually "gave place to brighter colour; there was less heather and more pasturage".

I descended on Carron from the north, through a humid languid atmosphere. The weather had cheated me. Loch Carron and its environs, which normally resemble a Norwegian fjord — and as such doubtless commended themselves to the Vikings — was no more stimulating than a kitchen on washing day. Was the climate better in Norse days than it was today? Or did the Vikings also become sickened of rain and frequently suffer from colds and chills?

There is far more to this district than tidal water and knobbly hills. Southey mentioned benevolent pasturelands, and corn is still grown. The light green spears of growth develop into the golden-yellow of high summer — gold to rival the blazing yellow of broom, which takes over from the gorse to light up the Highland year.

Indeed, the river Carron, in an amiable course from Dugall's Loch at Achnashellach, drains a fertile countryside. It sweeps to the loch between banks of shingle, massed gorse, and finally between sea-washed turf of a quality fit for a bowling green.

Walking from the lochside to the top of a hill could be like walking from summer back into spring. Red-throated divers adorn the lochans. A few ptarmigan, Arctic-type birds with frosty voices, inhabit the tops. Buckley, one of the old writers, told us that the Strath Carron was a regular breeding place for golden eagles. No-one harmed the birds. An eagle nest in an area where sticks were not easily obtained was assembled of heather stalks, lined and edged with fresh green heather. "This huge mass of material is placed on a ledge of rock generally having a northern aspect," added Buckley.

It was incongruous, in such remote and attractive surroundings, to be held up at a level crossing, part of the railway between Dingwall and Kyle — the most northerly rail system linking Scotland's east and west coasts. The Kyle line, crossing Scotland via Garve and Achnasheen, is reliable in most sorts of weather. Subsidised to the tune of some £200,000 a year, it refuses to die, and with the prospects for more and more people using it the chances of survival are good. Should there be oil-related developments near the mouth of Loch Carron, the line would be needed. Strange-looking loads would then be borne west, for the construction of oil-rig platforms has been mentioned.

The railway goes south of the water, being at first adjacent to a new road which made Strome ferry redundant. Road and rail share a concrete canopy near cliffs of such instability they are draped with ponderous wire netting. By its aid, the roadway is kept clear of small boulders, though avalanches have blocked the route for weeks at a time.

The railway is a good example of the verve, and nerve, of the Victorians. Constructed in the 1860s, it terminated at Stromeferry but was then extended to Kyle. Steamers carried passengers and goods on to Skye. (A steamer stolen from the company was found in Melbourne, Australia!) The Beeching Report of 1963 threatened the Kyle line with closure. Ten years later it was being reprieved for yet another year, and an action committee of interested people was claiming that the expenditure of capital on improvements might cut down the journey time across Scotland to about two hours.

From the new road by Carron I could scan marshland. One evening I went to the head of the loch. The tide, nearing its peak, had lost some of its boisterous nature on its way up from the open sea. Raised beaches around Carron testify, to those with informed eyes, that the sea-level was considerably higher during the closing phases of the Pleistocene period. One beach levels off at about 100 feet above the present water level.

My expedition, which began at Loch Carron, was delayed near the village. A red-breasted merganser floated near the shore, rising and falling with the waves in what must have been a sleep-inducing rhythm. Near it were patches of khaki weed, moving in unison with the bird and inducing drowsiness in the observer! I watched the bird's movements for a while, and then switched my attention to a heron hunting where the flow-tide had slackened, the water being calm.

The heron's eyes, set in a black-pennanted head, were fixed on the shallows but the bird was uneasy as I continued to survey it. Rising into the air on powder-blue wings, it added another fifty yards to the distance between us. Herons are quite common in western sea lochs, which offer the birds good feeding throughout the year.

The bridge was a good vantage point for viewing the riverside shingle, on which several pairs of gulls had nested. An oyster-catcher slunk off, hunch-backed, with head down. Blackbirds darted with fruity chuckles between thickets of gorse. Lesser redpolls, which are late nesters, circled with rippling trills.

From a tree ahead came an unfamiliar song – four or five fluted trochees. They formed a neat sequence of sound, clear and persistent, beginning at the top of the scale and descending. An interval of about a minute lay between the sequences. The songster was using a moderately tall tree as a perch, and a flare of light from the loch was behind it. identified the songster as a small thrush and saw, with mounting excitement, that this strange bird had a white eye stripe.

That evening, standing alone between untidy banks of gorse and a few trees in Wester Ross, I saw — for the first time in my experience — a redwing in its summer quarters. I had known the redwing well as a winter visitor, associating it with those other northern thrushes, the fieldfares. Hitherto I had heard only the sibilant call notes of redwings in passage. One late October evening, visiting in a West Riding mill town, I heard the flight calls of the 'taiga-thrush' as flocks flew high.

I had heard that redwings had bred in Scotland, first in the Moray basin, and now in parts of Sutherland and Inverness-shire. Wester Ross was stated to be one of their most favoured areas. Was the bird I saw just a singing male? Or one of a pair nesting in the area? Scanning some likely nesting places, low down in trees and shrubs, I disturbed only blackbirds. They rose and rocketed away, low down, with clattering shouts.

An angler confirmed my identification of the bird as a redwing. "You canna mistake its song," he declared. Then he switched our talk to his favourite topic — salmon. Some fine fish were lying in the pools before moving upriver to the spawning grounds with a freshet. Sea trout also follow the river Carron at spawning time.

The marshland extending beyond the mini-jungle of gorse was deeply indented, like a hand stretched out, fingers slightly apart. The last of the flow ran up the smooth-sided gutters; it also bit off pieces of marsh and would presumably return the eroded material elsewhere. The outline of marshland is never constant. What the tide takes today, the tide will surely return elsewhere on the morrow.

Waves broke across a promontory on which oystercatchers had assembled. Eiders, ducks and young, rode the choppy water. A few eiders that had clambered on to a bank found themselves, within minutes, on a diminishing islet. Displaced oystercatchers took flight, calling irritably.

Out in the loch were the long, low, streamlined forms of divers down from the hill lochans. The bodies were frequently concealed as the birds lay in troughs between the waves. None of the fine detail of their plumage could be seen in the poor light. On diving, they went completely from sight and I recalled a day spent by a bay the shore of which was a crescent of white sand. The high sun peered through transparent water to the very bed of the sea, and divers could be followed in their underwater progress after fish. How were the divers of Loch Carron faring now in a silt-laden water?

The marsh held a litter of debris — weed, empty mussel shells, a plastic toy and even the bleached skull of a cow. Mergansers called with gruff voices. A hooded crow departed. Its mandibles had a vice-like grip on a mussel. Where the marsh took the brunt of the tide, it had been broken up into pieces so small and rounded they were like green pin-cushions. A lapwing flew by, and a redshank yelled alarm — a clear "tui" that became a rippling medley as the bird alighted on shingle. Later in the summer, when waders from the far north had responded to the migration impulses, packs of sanderling and other birds would patter on these very beaches, collecting food borne in by the tide.

The village overlooking the sea loch was called Jeantown, but is now Lochcarron. Viewed from a high point of the southern shore of the loch, it gave the impression of being a string of white beads. A high rainfall is deflected from the houses by slate and tile, but within living memory there were several thatched cottages, presumably of the kind seen at Plockton, where an example of the everyday architecture of Old Scotland is now a much-photographed curiosity. Lochcarron's modern street lighting must surely have been based on that of Blackpool.

Robert Southey visited Jeantown when it was "chiefly or wholely inhabited by fishermen. A few of the huts on the shore are continguous; the much greater number stand separately upon the hill-side. A great part of the year the men, from the nature of their calling, have nothing to do; yet they buy their nets at Inverness, instead of employing some of their leisure hours in making them."

Fishing and farming, for long the twin pursuits along the western coastline, ended as a joint enterprise about 1850. Fishing depended on the appearance in Loch Carron of great herring shoals. By mid-century they no longer arrived. The number of visiting salmon and sea trout dwindled. From mid-century, too, the human population went into a steady decline. Nearly 5,000 people had lived in Jeantown and Applecross fifty years before.

Farming continues. Beef cattle still lumber about the hills, where the calves are born. Spring calving was the custom of a few years ago, but autumn calving is now commoner. Cattle do good to a hill. They take rough vegetation and fertilise the ground with their ample droppings. The beasts are wintered on the low ground.

After breakfasting, Robert Southey had "set off for Strome Ferry with the intention of crossing there if Applecross's new boat should be ready". The ferry, for long a feature of the Strome narrows, no longer operates. Its value ended with the coming of the new road. Southey's carriage, the first to reach the ferry, doubtless received immediate and special attention. In recent years a five-hour wait in high summer for passage with cars was stoically tolerated by visitors.

Travelling to Ardaneaskan, near the mouth of Loch Carron, I stopped at a junction and asked a pedestrian about the alternative roads. He replied: "Go 400 yards that way [towards the now-disused Strome ferry landing] and you'll find nothing. Go rather more than a mile that way [towards Ardaneaskan] and it's nothing again!" (I reflected that a similar comment might be made of Drumbuie, a lightly-populated shoulder of Loch Carron. Then the oil-boom, and a need for deep water to construct platforms threatened Drumbuie's way of life – life that had the impression of being changeless.)

The conifers of Strome Forest banded with morning shadows the road to Ardaneaskan, whose white-washed buildings stood adjacent to the foundations of former homes and outbuildings. It had clearly been a larger and busier place. Natives of Ardaneaskan emigrated to distant places, to Montana and New Zealand, as well as to the towns of lowland Britain. "Now here are young people wanting to come back," said a woman. 'They're sick of the towns. If they build oil rigs in Loch Carron, where will the workers live? Houses are in short supply — and very pricey. There's a terrible lot of second homes."

The road ended with an informal parking area overlooking the sea. House sparrows chirped on the thatch of a former barn, and eiders polka-dotted the sea. I was told that bracken was frequently used for outbuildings, but heather — which was considered superior material — was set in place on dwellings. Heather is short-stemmed, and presumably the thatchers of old gathered it with roots and plenty of adherent peat, which would act as a binding material.

The smooth surface of the bay, 100 yards offshore, was disturbed by a cruising seal — a grey seal. The main Hebridean breeding station of the species is North Rona. The sighting of a seal once caused a ripple of excitement in the district. From a grey seal corpse came food, clothing and lamp-oil. Modern requirements are obtained, pre-packed, from any local store!

I viewed Loch Carron from the new road on the southern shore. A raven drifted by, high up. The new road led me into another new forest. When the road broke clear, I saw a cuckoo perched on a wire strung across the road. This bird fascinated me for it was disinclined to fly. Was the cuckoo attached by quicklime?

The cuckoo's manner was explained when I observed a male buzzard sweeping a hillside about fifty yards away. A female buzzard, perched on a telegraph pole about fifty yards from me in the other direction, preened its feathers, then raised a foot, lowered its head and briskly cleaned its beak. The buzzards departed, pitching down at the edge of a plantation. The cuckoo, which had doubtless been waiting for them to go, flew off.

A raggle-taggle of birch and coarse vegetation lay beside the road to Plockton. 'Plock', which is Gaelic, meaning a small hilly promontory, aptly sums up the situation of one of Scotland's prettiest villages.

South Strome Forest, seen from Plockton across water dotted with eider, included superb native Scots pines, and thus held on to the atmosphere of Old Caledonia. Such pines must have stood all round Loch Carron when the Norsemen came to this splendid area in their clinker-built craft with dragonesque prows and striped mainsails.

If they returned on a summer week-end they would need their wits about them to avoid hitting some of an armada of holiday boats!

6

DEER ON THE HILL

To be sure of seeing red deer, I had to climb high — to the misty corries, alpine meadows and the high ridges. Here, by day, one might see red stags in recline. They needed prolonged peaceful conditions to complete the complicated digestive processes that convert fresh herbage into nourishment for their bodies and sustain the new antler growth.

Many of the hinds, at slightly lower elevations, and having calves at foot, were super-sensitive to the sights and sounds and smells around them. Several times, when trying to close with hinds, I heard the gruff bark of alarm from a nervous matron.

I watched creatures that were in the Highlands long before man. The vanguard of red deer crossed a land bridge connecting Britain with the Continent. As the effects of glaciation eased, the red deer could move farther and farther north. About 7,000 years have gone by since the noble animals established themselves in the Highland fauna. They were huge animals compared with today's stock. Man debased the landscape, and consequently the size of the deer that depended upon it. Today a Highland stag may be only about half the size and weight of a stag of the same species cosetted in an English deer park or of one of its Continental cousins.

Spring had been late in the year of my Highland jaunt. The upland pastures, with cold rain and wind upon them, did not begin to show a first great flush of grass until May, even June in places. Summer was slow to reveal itself. Even in late June usually a bright and beneficial part of the year — with the protein content of lowland grass not far past its peak — located low-lying areas near villages where red deer grazed at dusk.

The deer moved into view hesitantly, with suspicion, as well they might, near the haunts of men. Then, continuing boldly, they snatched at a few mouthfuls of herbage on their way to the lush flats by river or burn. While humans slept, the deer devoted themselves to several hours of steady grazing.

Man has taken over from the wolf pack the role of main predator on deer. He became the most dangerous predator of all. Highland reds had learnt by long experience how to cope with the wolf, which claimed mainly the old, the young and the infirm. The wolf, which did not seriously threaten the existence of the deer as a local species, became extinct in the Highlands about 1745.

Man largely destroyed the Highland forest canopy, though it is theorised that red deer were primarily creatures of the forest edge, not true woodlanders. They ventured on to warm and open hillsides during the short summer, but needed forest food and shelter in hard weather. With the trees gone from most areas, they were now forced to endure the open hill continuously.

Now conifer forests are ringed by deer-proof fencing. Lochs dammed by water authorities, and those concerned with the provision of electricity from water-power, have extended over former low country grazings. In days of high meat prices, poaching is prevalent. Defensive mechanisms that were developed by the red deer over long ages, to cope with the wolf, are of little value when deer are stalked by men carrying high powered rifles, as they do even in summer when some animals, classed as 'marauders', will be destroyed.

A wild deer lives for the moment. It does not reflect on past events. Nor does it (as far as we know) ponder on the future. The red deer I watched in the West Highlands were contented deer, with abundant fresh food to consume. Forgotten, forever, were the privations of winter and spring.

An oldish stag living on the hills near Loch Carron was still in unsightly moult when red deer in English parks had the full summer coat upon them. The Highlander showed the smooth, lustrous summer coat in those places from which tufts of old hair had fallen. The general effect, however, was that the animal was wearing a favourite but threadbare jersey!

Deer in temperate zones do not retain their summer coat for long; it fades, indeed, before the season ends. At a time of year which holidaymakers fondly imagine to be summer, the Highland reds may be already showing traces of the winter coat to come!

The Loch Carron stag had an impressive growth of new horn under nutrient velvet that, when the horn growth was complete, would dry and strip off. I recall the stag's long, even trot — a haughty locomotion, with head well up and legs stiffened. Watching the deer leap down to the bed of a burn, and go out of my sight, I saw a creamy rump patch, against which was revealed the light-brown tail.

I inquired about deer in every locality I visited. There were many but "they've gone to the hill". I must follow them on high. By gaining elevation, the deer escape from the worst ravages of the insects that teem on low, wet ground. No mammal likes to have insects buzzing around its head, and burgeoning new antlers of deer are porous, almost spongy, and easily damaged. A bite from an insect on the soft tissue may be so severe it will endure — as a mark on the hard antler!

In summer, midges, clegs, gadflies and a host of other insects cause great irritation to wild creatures. Particularly abnoxious is the black-and-yellow nostril fly, which hovers around the nostrils of a deer and, briefly touching down, ejects into the nostrils a fluid containing larvae. These attach themselves to the nasal cavity and develop, to be sneezed out by the frantic deer in the following spring.

Comfort from heat as well as insect pests drives deer to plunge their hot bodies into the burns. Or they wallow churning up peat and water into a porridge-like mixture and emerging dark and dripping, soon to dry out again in the warm breezes. Cairngorm deer, climbing to around or above 4,000 feet, lie happily in banks of snow.

To John Colquhoun (1888) a wallow was a "forest-bath" or a "moss hole". The stags "plunge up to the neck and roll about to cool themselves . . . When they come out again, black a pitch, they look like the evil genii of the mountain." Years ago, according to Colquhoun, poachers fastened spears with the points upwards in the wallows, "and when the stag threw himself into the hole, he was impaled". Peter Delap has written about wallows sited at traditional points on lines of travel. He theorised that originally they may have provided olfactory camouflage from the pursuing wolf pack.

Parties of hinds occupy the 'middle ground' in summer (and descend only marginally lower on the hill in winter). The peak time for calving is mid-June. A calf develops in the soft, moist comfort of the womb during a winter and spring in which the hind itself may have been in extremis, scrambling over icy rocks or being stung by blizzards.

When calving time is near, a hind begins to show a distinct lack of interest in the youngster to which it gave birth in the previous year. The yearling, puzzled by the conduct of its parent, wanders disconsolately until, in due course, with the new calf active, the hind accepts it back. Young stags tend to stay with the hind parties for a year or two. In June those coming up to an age of three years drift away to be absorbed by the group of males on higher land.

A hillside may look bare, but the hind knows where to drop the new calf to provide it with maximum cover. It may be a tract of heather or simply a tuft of rushes. The calf 'freezes' to such good effect that strangers, coming across it accidentally, have taken it to be asleep, an impression seen to be false if a calf is picked up (which it should never be) and becomes shrilly vocal. It has for long been believed that a new deer calf has no scent detectable by potential enemies.

The infant mortality is high — as much as 50 per cent. Golden eagles take a few calves. So do the foxes. The weather has a major influence on success at calving time. Cold, wet weather draggles the hair of new-born calves, which thus become chilled. The hind does what it can to provide shelter, and there is nourishment, too, in the milk it offers, which is about six times as nourishing as the milk given by the modern cow.

I never look for calves. Go out with the specific task of finding them, and you will be frustrated. I have, however, found calves accidentally during summer walks on the hills. A calf lies flat out, screened by vegetation. Long ears are folded backwards from a head that has a domed forehead. There is a short muzzle, glistening with good health. The solidity of the body form is 'broken up' by a dappled coat, though the spots quickly fade, leaving a coat of dull brown. A two-day old calf, if healthy, can run more quickly than a man. Youngsters join up and disport themselves in games, like lambs. They bounce along as though each foot had a spring attached to it.

Grim hill conditions have long since decreed that it is better for a red deer to rear a single calf than to attempt to-bring up twins. Instances of twins are rare. A case occurred on the island of Rhum in October 1970, the sire being a hummel. One calf was a male, the other female, and each weighed 13½ pounds at birth. It was, of course, a late birth, and if born in the wild the calves would almost certainly have been lost during the following winter.

Within an hour of birth, the calf has been cleaned up and suckled. It is left alone, but the hind does not go far. A distress call from the calf brings help. Normally, the hind returns to its calf three times a day, and it is presumed that it lies with the new calf during the brief summer night. Our knowledge of a deer's nocturnal activities is sparse.

A hind must not overdraw on its strength. It may be three even four years old before the first calf is produced. The hind may then miss breeding in one year (when it is 'yeld') while producing a lusty calf in the year following.

Before summer ends, the older stags have shed their velvet and new horns are revealed — horns that become dark and burnished as the animals rub them against the ground or tree. Rich summer feeding brings the stags into peak condition. An increasing irritability indicates that another rutting time approaching. The haunts on the high hills are vacated for the rutting grounds as summer gives way to autumn.

7

MAM RATAGAN

The modern Road to the Isles thrusts for 56 miles between Invermoriston and the Kyle of Lochalsh, from which large ships sail to Skye. I joined the Road after travelling on single-track ways that had run amiably, conforming to the whims of topography, through a region holding far more deer than people. Only 1,200 folk reside in the area between the lochs of Carron, Alsh and Duich.

Now I was jarred by traffic on the much-improved main tourist route to the coast. The Road was impressive — awesome, indeed — in its disregard of the rocky terrain. It was, without doubt, a considerable engineering effort. The invoice for explosives used should be framed in a Highland museum. A vehicle could overtake another without recourse to a 'passing place', ending the age of chivalry. Car and caravan tyres strum on a silk-smooth surface.

A holidaymaker who had drawn his car off the road at a point near Dornie was recovering from the peculiar fatigue of being a tourist — pricking eyes, stiff back, sluggish bowels. Soon his children were sucking the promised ice lollies. A transistor radio blared. A youth carrying heavy pack and guitar strode towards Kyle, and so intent was he on his destination that when he thumbed vehicles he simply listened for their approach, then raised an arm without looking round. He seemed reconciled to being ignored.

Had the native people gone to ground? Only one of them attracted attention. A solitary piper stood by the castle of Eilean Donan – island castle a photograph of which is compulsory for all Scottish calendars — and he tried to instil some authentic Highland music into a foreign babble. The piper wore full Highland dress. The strains of his pipes were soulful, lying heavy on the still air.

Eilean Donan, in its superb position, must be worth thousands of pounds a year to the manufacturers of colour film. Here cameras are operated like machine guns. The name of the castle is derived from Donnan, a Celtic monk — one time Abbot of Eigg — whose activities, recounted verbally down the centuries, have acquired the moss of imaginative story-telling. Such tales help to sustain the West Highland melancholia.

There *was* sadness in the life of Donnan. He died in such a way he was bound to be remembered. While celebrating Mass beside Loch Duich on Easter day, A.D. 617, he was interrupted by pirates; they made a prisoner of the saint and fifty-two of his monks, pronouncing the death penalty, which would be delayed until the celebration of the Mass was concluded. Surely no man had greater cause to linger over the sacrament. When it was completed, Donnan was beheaded.

Eilean Donan broods at the confluence of Lochs Alsh, Long and Duich. I reached the place after crossing a bridge at Dornie. Older people remember when one used a ferryboat. I saw podgy eider riding a flow tide into which terns plunge dived for fish, the birds otherwise circling with creaky voices.

The destruction of the old castle came from the sea. In Jacobite times, three English warships sailed up Loch Alsh and bombarded the fortress, then manned by a Spanish garrison supervised by the fifth Earl of Seaforth (one of the Mackenzies of Kintail). Eilean Donan lay ruined until the period between 1912 and 1930, when Colonel Macrae-Gilstrap restored the place so sensitively and completely it might never have been harmed. It was not just an exercise in nostalgia — a desire to turn back the clock. Included in the years of patient restoration were the terrible slump years, and castle-building gave work to otherwise jobless men.

I viewed the castle from the high road that served local and tourist needs for many years until the new road was blasted from the rock along Duich's northern shore. Then I turned to

(above) Eider duck brooding its eggs

(below) Newly-hatched eider ducklings

Plockton, by Loch Carron

scan the hills. There was a small number of beef cattle in sight. Kintail was especially noted for its cattle until a Highland tragedy occurred, local families being displaced by the landowners to make way for large-scale sheep farming. The MacRaes, among those who suffered eviction, are still referred to as 'the scattered children of Kintail'.

The newcomers were mainly farmers from southern Scotland. They supervised sheep walks established in the Glens of Shiel, Elchaig and Lichd at a time when the emigrants from Kintail were adjusting themselves to life in foreign parts. The less resourceful families, who had not left the Highlands, huddled at the edge of the sea and lived by the proceeds of fishing and farming — of a sort. Sheep completed the devastation of the landscape, a process that had begun with the felling of native woods.

I followed the Road from the Isles, going eastwards and crossing a causeway to pass through a cutting in which the raw stone had a pinkish hue. The whine and whoosh of traffic was continuous, so I turned towards the road which, though improved, has not lost its wild spirit, making a bold frontal assault on Mam Ratagan. The way led to Glenelg, from which a ferry sails across an uneasy channel to Skye. It was used by Dr Johnson and his friend Boswell in 1773.

Mam Ratagan's road has a gradient of 1 in 6 and zig-zags through a conifer forest. The motorist ascends 1,200 feet in three miles. Ironically, on one stretch when the car was labouring and its bonnet was lined up with the sky I had to apply the brakes. Sharing the limited road-space was a timber wagon, a titan that faced me from a range of a dozen yards as I swept round a bend.

On the climb, I was blinkered by conifers and envied the travellers of the 1930s who saw the district before close views were blotted out by trees. Mine was a twilight journey. The trees soared until their tops were well outside my normal field of vision; I was dimly aware of branches and foliage high above. Then, from a parking space at the top of the pass, I watched cloud patches sneaking between the hills. Northwards lay a range of majestic peaks, the Five Sisters of Kintail, grey under mist, huddling as though for mutual comfort.

My road dipped into Glenelg, and trees petered out. The forest gave way to a fertile glen, though a few Scots pines clung indomitably to an exposed hill. Black-faced sheep, with well-grown lambs at foot, claimed part of the road. Down by the sea stood a church, bar, ferry boat — and a shingle beach. The war memorial was pointed out with pride, having cost £6,000. Its position, with a view of a restless channel and the lesser hills of Skye, was by itself worth that money.

A cul-de-sac road, resembling a doodle on the map, serves Eileanreach, Sandaig and Arnisdale, which is *Ring of Bright Water* country. Who, having read Gavin Maxwell's bitter-sweet book, can forget the basic elements of an area in which a man's craving for a solitary life amid great natural beauty was satisfied? Maxwell lived at 'Camusfearna', and "nowhere in all the West Highlands and Isles have I seen a place of so intense and varied beauty in so small a compass". As the world now knows, he befriended otters. Arguably, otters befriended him. The flutelike whistle of the otter may still be heard in the district at dusk.

Edal, the most famous otter, died years ago and its remains lie under a cairn not far from a rock slab marking the site of 'Camusfearna', a house destroyed under the terms of Maxwell's will. Under another slab of rock are the ashes of the author, yet this sensitive man achieved a degree of immortality. The man, his home and his otters have gone, but *A Ring of Bright Water* will endure.

Back to Glenelg's costly war memorial. I scanned the quarter of a mile of turbulent water between the mainland and Skye here in one of its least dramatic quarters. Each autumn, long ago, about 6,000 cattle from the island were set to swim across a stretch of tidal fury where I could not imagine any mammal surviving for long. Presumably, the drovers were experts on the tide and weather. The cattle were beginning their long journey to the English markets. A fanciful story insists that the ferrymen tied a noose around the tail of one beast and attached the other end of the rope to the lower jaw of the animal following. It seemed a pointless exercise, calling for considerable time, patience — and innumerable pieces of rope!

Cattle, brisk and fat after the rich summer grazing on Skye, emerged from the sea in steaming droves, to be controlled by men and dogs who would be away from home for weeks at a time and who, in succeeding weeks, had to adjust their pace and temperaments to that of the stock. It was a long trek southwards — and then those in charge had to walk home again!

The drovers were gamblers. They gambled on the stock remaining safe and healthy, and also on the state of the market. Cattle disease periodically spread through the herds, and one drover, Thomas Bell, wrote after an expedition: "I am positive we have lost three thousand pounds already. I shall be home at Candlemas, and people may do with me as they will. They shall get every groat we have, and we can do no more."

When I stopped in Glen Beg to see a waterfall that was roaring out like a prophet in the wilderness, there were cattle in view. What sort of stock was owned by the Iron Age folk of over 2,000 years ago who inhabited this very glen? And did individual men find time to stop and stare, as I had done, at the tumbling water?

The folk of the Iron Age were not rough savages; they had great social awareness and some sophistication, as evidenced by their building techniques. The brochs of Glen Beg date from about that time.

A broch is a large circular structure, with galleries set in hollow walls and stone staircases linking one gallery to another. The broch was more than a home. Here people found refuge in time of trouble. It must have been the equivalent of the pele tower of northern England, though this was a much later model. Glen Beg has the finest examples of brochs on mainland Scotland. At a time of multi-storied building and other architectural elaborations, these brochs still have the power to impress by their size and worthiness.

I returned to the Road to the Isles with caution as well as misgivings, but soon its charm had captivated me. Scenery on a grand scale enveloped me as I journeyed through Glen Shiel, of which an early Victorian traveller wrote: "The mountains, with their peaked and fretted tops and scanty vegetation, tower up piercing the clouds. A limpid stream gurgles among the rocks at the bottom of the valley, and the road winds gracefully by its side down the glen."

Similar sensations of awe and veneration had been enjoyed sixty years earlier by the ebullient Dr Johnson. This region was "not very flowery, but sufficient verdant". The doctor travelled this way in autumn — as did many early tourists — and it was here that he decided to record his impressions of the Highlands for possible publication. The horses needed food and rest, said the guides, who "intreated us to stop here, because no grass would be found in any other place. The request was reasonable, and the argument cogent. We therefore willingly dismounted and diverted ourselves as the place gave us opportunity."

Johnson sat on a bank "such as a writer of romance might have delighted to feign. I had indeed no trees to whisper over my head, but a clear rivulet streamed at my feet. The day was calm, the air soft, and all was rudeness, silence and solitude. Before me, and on either side, were high hills which, by hindering the eye from ranging, forced the mind to find entertainment for itself. Whether I spent the hour well I know not; for here I first conceived the thought of this narration."

Beyond the deep confines of Loch Shiel were broad views — of sparkling water, new forests, a vast sky. The forest land, a dark green carpet with a thick pile, had that sort of tight uniformity that nature, left to itself, would abhor. With time and infinite patience I might have located a pine marten, now reportedly spreading southwards from the rocky fastnesses that gave it sanctuary when the old forest cover was removed by man. Other mammals are spreading northwards. Sika deer, of Asiatic origin, introduced into the Highlands for sport, have reached Glen Moriston from the vicinity of Loch Ness. Th wildcat prowls in Glen Moriston, and roe deer, for long — like the marten — forced to endure conditions on the open hill, have slipped as inconspicuously as shadows under the canopy of the new forests.

Fort Augustus, which I reached that afternoon, is a pretentious English name for a settlement that was anciently known as Cill Chumin, after Cummein, the seventh abbot of Iona. He wrote a tract dealing with miracles performed by St Columba, who made several protracted and hazardous journeys through the province of the Picts, following the Great Glen to the Pictish capital of Inverness. It is a journey now made with ease and comfort by the motorist.

Columba would have to struggle with rank vegetation and marshes. A boat would presumably have been used for much of the journey, using the several lochs that later were exploited for the grand canal. Columba, crossing the river Ness, saw the funeral procession of a swimmer who had been seized by a 'monster'. The saint demonstrated the power of the Faith when he asked a spectator to swim across the river and collect a boat beached on the other side. Naturally, the swimmer attracted the monster's attention, but Columba — invoking God's name — instructed the beast to withdraw, which it did! The courageous swimmer collected the boat and returned, safely, to the near bank.

That incident occurred in the sixth century. Ten centuries later, monsters still lurked at Loch Ness. An unidentified animal of great size was reported to have come ashore and felled trees by sweeping its tail. Three onlookers were killed. None of the 'kelpies', or water creatures, in Northern Britain, was to achieve such notoriety, or be glamorised to such an extent, as the Loch Ness Monster. We all thrive on sensations, and enjoy tales of Nessie.

Loch Ness is an imposing arena for tales of mystery. Twenty-four miles long, and with a width varying up to one and a half miles, it has a maximum depth of nearly 1,000 feet. Loch Ness was remote to visitors until the new road was cut (quite literally cut out in places) from Inverness to Fort Augustus. Even today, few people live around the loch. Few people venture near its shores, except at Urquhart Castle, a former stronghold of the Grants, which is open to public inspection. Most sightings of the monster have been reported near this spot.

That evening I ran the risk of being attacked by the monster, I walked on the shore of Loch Ness. A mist that was stained salmon pink by filtered sunlight hung about the loch. If a trout had risen within a quarter of a mile I must surely have seen it, for the water was to all intents and purposes static.

No monster rose to view. No weird screams were heard from visitors under attack. I wondered what Columba and his monks would have thought of the sika deer now inhabiting the woods. The sika is not of monstrous size, and its appearance gives the impression that it has been assembled from several species of deer. It has the simple branched antlers of the red deer, the body size and height of a fallow, and an impressive amount of caudal white, such as the roe bears.

The sika's voice, heard in unenlightened times, would have given rise to stories of a monster. It is a slate-pencil type of squeal that sounds, from a distance, like a whistle — or the piping of a northern Pan. A stag during the rut, calling in the half-light — sometimes deep in the night — utters three loud squeals. One cannot anticipate them. There might be twenty minutes or so between sequences. A human standing near a vocal animal feels his scalp prickle. A sex-crazed stag sometimes begins to squeal but ends with an agonised groan.

Enduring legends are made of outbursts like these!

8

THE SUNSET COAST

Kenneth MacLeod's tramping song, "Road to the Isles", was in my mind during a drive westwards from Fort Augustus to Fort William. I had sampled the early stages of that old Road, "by Tummel and Loch Rannoch and Lochaber"; I had trudged "by heather tracks wi' heaven in their wiles". Now I must go "in blithely forward marching time" (which is how MacLeod wanted his song to be rendered) "by Ailort and by Morar to the sea . . .".

The Road was used by drovers. This way, in autumn, came a tangy, snorting host of black cattle from the islands, attended by men toughened by Highland life. The stock was delivered to lowland trysts, from which it went, on further long pedestrian stages, to the markets of England. Wales and Ireland also supplied beef on the hoof, but the Scots contribution in meeting need for protein by the English townsman is remembered through song as well as prose.

Drove roads lay on my native Pennines. Visiting a farm in Upper Teesdale, I heard Scotch cattle referred to as 'kyloes', a term derived from the fact that cattle had first to swim the kyles from island to mainland.

There was time, during my wearisome journey westwards in the Great Glen, among tourist traffic, to daydream about recent experiences "by Tummel and Loch Rannoch". First I climbed a hill near Pitlochry to where lapwings called as they tumbled over a large re-seeded meadow. The plaintive cries of birds anxious about their young were associated, in Gaelic folk lore, with lost souls.

Brown hares grazed in a field of young grain. One of them

tuned its ears to the local wavelengths, also rearing on its hind legs as though to peer around. The five-inch-long ears twisted and turned like sensitive radar scanners. So intense was the animal's concentration I felt it must surely hear me breathe. The farmer had found three leverets huddled in the nursery form, and yet another — a larger — leveret with a sprinkling of dry grasses across it, a form of camouflage for which the doe must have been responsible. Hitherto he had found single leverets, not a whole family together.

Does the doe, as is asserted by some, deliberately pick up leverets with its mouth, transferring them to forms scattered about the area, so that only one at a time might be found by enemies? Or is the explanation of the dispersal of the young to be found in the precociousness of the leverets? Do they adventurously move out from an early age? Leverets need to make an early bid for independence. A doe will visit each of its young at least twice in twenty-four hours, but the suckling season for each litter is short.

A leveret immediately threatened by a predator squeals and jumps high, to alert the doe, which has the courage at such times to drive off quite large predators. A friend imitated the leveret squeal at dusk. Moments later a brown owl lighted on a post a few yards from it, attracted, no doubt, by a faint chance of food!

The brown hare of our pastures and meadows was a comparative latecomer to the British scene. The mountain or blue hare was here first, during the closing phases of the Ice Ages. By the time the brown hare came, the land link with Ireland had gone. The 'Irish hare' was already in Ireland. The brown hare reached that country through introductions by sportsmen.

Later in my walk above Pitlochry, a tuft of grass had erupted to disgorge another hare — an eight-pound creature that was almost two feet long from nose to tail. Total immobility is one way in which the brown hare escapes detection. Disturb it, and it springs from cover and demonstrates a startling burst of speed from a crouching start. The hare needs a prolonged and preferably undisturbed daytime rest. Then its complex digestive processes can be adequately completed before, with the coming of another night, it goes forth to feed once more.

Conifers smothered the upper part of the hill above Pitlochry. I followed one of the rides, seeing a roe doe cross and then being loudly cursed by a roebuck. Gruff and loud, uttered by a beast that cannot have been more than twenty yards away, but had the benefit of full tree cover, the bark sounded from time to time, with diminishing effect, as the roebuck departed.

A doe had left the forest to graze a re-seeded field. On that spring evening there was an indication of its summer beauty. Basically the doe was in winter coat, but a reddening of the neck, foreparts and legs was detectable. The moult was under way. In a week or two the roe would look brilliant, clad in hair of foxy red.

I also recalled, during my drive down the Great Glen, towards the Sunset Coast, an afternoon I spent by Rannoch. Cuckoos frequently called as I walked on the hills near the Black Wood. The Rannoch-side cuckoos flaunted themselves before my gaze. One was perched on an electricity wire; another on the ground, near some sheep and gulls. With its soft grey plumage and lyrical call, the cuckoo may give an impression that it lacks stamina, but it is quite common on the exposed Highland hillsides. I have heard cuckoos calling at dawn in a world whitened by hoar frost. Another bird, using a fencing post as a perch when the district was being swept by a shower of sleet, looked lively even though spring had been temporarily banished. I looked at the bird through binoculars and noticed a beady droplet of moisture dangling from its beak!

Another spring sound by Loch Rannoch was the soprano voice of the blackfaced lamb, to which was added from time to time the contralto bleating of the ewe. I found a group of sheep grazing a stretch of turf — an oblong of emerald green in a frame that was of dun-colour. The rest of the hill was still in a winter lethargy.

Four golden plover, clad in the nuptial black and gold, took mincing steps before flicking their way aloft on thin, angled wings. A curlew — the 'whaup' of Old Scotland — drawled as it glided. A cock wheatear "chacked".

On my return to Loch Rannoch I watched storms moving by in dour procession, to be enlivened by the gleaming translucence of rainbows. It was restive weather. The hills were patched with sunshine and shadow. Some distant peaks had a tone of powder blue.

I saw a fly-past of black grouse, a species common enough on the hills around Tummel and Rannoch but quite scarce now in the west. Osgood Mackenzie of Gairloch lamented their loss. He wrote: "Along the shores of Loch Maree, my mother once counted 60 blackcock on the stooks of a very small field, and the old farmer, to whom the patch of oats belonged, told her he had counted one hundred the previous evening."

The Rannochside birds were in informal groups, flying quickly about fifty feet from the ground, showing off the broad white bars on dark wings. For the blackcock, the spring day begins early, with hissing and cooing at the display ground, the 'lek', where the birds indulge in ritualistic combat. The largest, boldest, most assertive birds claim the hens.

In the old days, droves of cattle using the Road from the Isles followed traditional ways across the empty moor of Rannoch. travelled as far as Rannoch station, which serves passengers on the railway crossing the eastern side of the moor. The station was under thick cloud and being pelted by rain, but a few stags were seen dimly.

A friend who lodged in those parts in his youth one evening in October went to the telephone kiosk after dark to call up a friend at Fort William. Stags were roaring so loudly, and from such close range, he excused himself, went outside the kiosk and hurled stones towards the stags in a vain attempt to silence them.

So much for daydreams! Now I was on the road to Fort William, and from here to Mallaig. A jay-walking sheep was a reminder that in the droving days sheep as well as cattle took the long, hard route to the markets. Larkin (1819) met large flocks that were being driven to the Falkirk tryst. Cattle drove

moved from Morvern in Argyllshire, and from the coastline and
islands of Wester Ross.

Larkin saw that the greater part of the cattle and sheep were
small. "Many of the former were lean, and some of them ill-
shaped, a bad property which does not usually belong to the
cattle of the western coast."

The broad road that swept out of Fort William towards
Mallaig degenerated to its old winding self just beyond the pulp
mill. More stretches were being improved farther on.

Tourists had taken over Glenfinnan, at the head of Loch
Shiel. They clustered round a baroque-style tower that is
surmounted by a sculpture of a Highlander — a memorial
relating to the heartache of the Forty-five, which is still felt in
the Highlands as though it were yesterday. The tract of land
round the memorial, sacred to those who love to think of the
auld' days, has been owned since 1938 by the National Trust
for Scotland. Here the Prince raised his standard in August
1745, and here a descendant of one of Charlie's supporters paid
for a memorial, which was constructed in 1815.

My road climbed, levelled out near Loch Eilt and descended
towards Loch Ailort. The two lochs, one of fresh water, the
other salty, are connected by one of the short, sharp, fast-
flowing western rivers beloved of sea trout at spawning time.
Salmon also use the river.

Sea trout, I was told, are moving upriver from May to July.
The first fish to appear are usually the heaviest of the year. An
average weight is given as eight pounds, but a sea trout
weighing twenty-one pounds has been landed. Sea trout spend
less time in the river than do salmon. I was told they apparently
do not journey far in the sea, reaching only the Faeroes,
whereas salmon move on to the plankton-rich waters off
Greenland.

An angler with a regard for sea trout thinks longingly of such
lochs as Eilt, Maree and Stack in Sutherland. Chatting with
one of the fishermen, I heard of his preferences when seeking
trout — windy conditions by day (he usually had his wish, even
in summer!) but calm conditions at night. Given these

circumstances, he said he could fill a boat with sea trout!

Do the migrant fish stop to investigate cages that have been suspended in the topmost reach of Loch Ailort? If so, they will come face to face with cossetted salmon that, hatched out in freshwater tanks, were brought to Ailort to be fed on special foods until they were of saleable size and condition. The timing when moving salmon from fresh to salt-water conditions must be 'just right'.

Those platforms in the loch appeared to be a focal point for birds. Local eiders take mussels growing on the floating structures. Precautions have been taken to stop cormorants entering the cages and gorging themselves on the pricey salmon. I watched a hooded crow alight on a cage with a reverberating "bonk". Hoodies are also fond of mussels, but unlike the eider — which can crack a shell — the birds must first drop mussels on to rocks to break them open.

Herons were working the edges of Loch Ailort. They, the cormorants that struck heraldic poses while perched on rocks between fishing trips, and the calm misty air, combined to form a pictorial effect that was Chinese in character. Yet on days when the wind zips from the open sea, Ailort can be driven into a fury, its waters piling up and restricting the flow of the river which frequently runs bank-high. In such conditions one spring I watched a great northern diver swimming in a flurry of water. Birds of this species that were reared in Greenland and Iceland appear in Scottish waters.

In summer, it is good to emulate the deer — to leave the valleys and trudge across the hills which are near but so remote from them in spirit. Red deer move in misted corries. One hears the belching call of the ptarmigan, which dear old Osgood Mackenzie of Gairloch called the white grouse. The ptarmigan has a brownish body in summer, but retains the wintry look. White is the winter garb, and white feathers adorn the bird's underparts and wings throughout the year, which is a good reason for its disinclination to fly far. Flashing white must draw a predator's attention.

To find a sitting ptarmigan calls for luck as well as skill. The bird, cryptically patterned, squats on a clutch of from five to nine eggs. The hen undertakes the incubation, but both hen and cock look after the chicks. These, lusty and precocious, are airborne in less than a fortnight! A few ptarmigan grace the tops of hills in the west. Osgood Mackenzie lamented their disappearance from old haunts. "From many hills that used to hold them — our own hill of about 2,600 feet included — the White Grouse has completely vanished," he wrote.

A chronicler of wild life today will notice that some species have greatly increased their numbers. The gull family has thrived. Great black-backed gulls nest beside hill lochans above Ailort. The bird is handsome, with a jet-black mantle and wings, the rest of the immaculate plumage being white. Rising on wings that span five and a half feet, the great black-backed gull calls "agh-agh" in a deep bass voice.

It was a novelty for local naturalists early this century when a pair of this largest, most terrifying, of the gull species nested on an islet in Loch Eilt and reared young. An angler who wrote enthusiastically about the birds considered they ornamented the scene. The eggs laid in the following season were destroyed, and the same angler rushed for his pen to denounce the vandal who "has deprived others of what was a pleasure every day, when the birds and their young were there".

Those who follow only the well-known routes through the Highlands can have little awareness of the vast tracts of land between the major glens. Unknown Scotland can begin a few hundred yards from a busy motor road. The Ardnish peninsula, beyond the railway line from Ailort to Mallaig, is one such area. Woods stand ankle-deep in bracken. Ruined buildings testify to the former profitable state of farming on what is now mainly sheep ground.

The way to Mallaig touched the edge of the open sea at Arisaig, where road and railway turned northward. In summer, when there is luxurious growth of vegetation, the district looks sub-tropical; there are even palm trees, thriving on the effects of the North Atlantic Drift. The Sound of Arisaig bustles with birds. I was told that in July 1960 no less than 1,000

Manx shearwaters were present.

I had entered that part of the coast where silica sand is backed by dunes thatched with marram and other pioneering grasses. White sands give continual brightness to the Morar district, and also light in tone are birches along the shore, the tree trunks being patterned, silver and black.

Swallows were working for insects across Loch Morar, which is the deepest freshwater loch in Scotland. A'Mhorag, a strange beast, used to appear to presage the death of a MacDonald of Morar.

A whimsical friend tells of Morar's contribution to the war effort. When 'heavy water' was needed for atomic research, a bucket with a lid was lowered on a rope into the deepest part of the loch, some 180 fathoms. When the bed was reached, the bucket lid was opened, then shut again. The bucket was drawn to the surface. "It was bound to contain heavy water," says my friend. "The heaviest water naturally lies at the bottom of the loch. There's nowhere deeper than Morar!"

I descended to Mallaig. Post office buildings had sprouted equipment connected with the radio telephone link with the islands, some of which were now in full view. Among them, brooding under cloud, was my destination — the island of Rhum.

9

A TYSTIE'S WORLD

A black guillemot, keeping station off the rocky shore, needless of the wave action and the wind-induced currents, looked so dumpy I first mistook it for a fisherman's buoy. Then the bird dived; it stayed underwater for almost a minute and bobbed into view, the plumage taking a faint gleam from the sunlight.

Black guillemot is known in the Shetlands as 'tystie' after its wheezy voice — a call that is pitched high but can be easily missed where the sea is booming and the shingle hisses. T.A. Coward called the voice "dreary and whining".

I first came to know the bird through the writings of E.A. Armstrong, who watched birds mainly along the coast of Antrim. Among them was the black guillemot, "A quaint, jolly little fellow . . . . The more you know him, the queerer and more likeable you find him to be." Years ago, the black guillemot nested off the east coast as far down as Yorkshire; it is now a bird seen most frequently off the north and west. Scotland has most of the estimated 8,000 or so birds frequenting British waters; I have also seen black guillemots afloat off the red sandstone cliffs of St Bees Head, Cumberland.

One evening, as I walked beside Loch Ailort (it was, I recall, a grey but calm evening, with the tide almost full) a tystie arrived with swift, low flight. The wings were being beaten so swiftly they were blurred to my sight and must surely have been buzzing. I saw the guillemot's red feet extending widely behind the body. Tystie held up its wings for a moment on alighting, and then tucked them neatly away.

They were short but broad wings, offering the bird more dexterous flight than that available to its cousin, the common guillemot, a bird which prefers at nesting time to pack cliff ledges overlooking the sea. Incidentally, the common guillemot is well-named in the British context. Over half a million birds of this species nest round our coasts.

Seeing the tystie bob prettily on Loch Ailort, a dozen miles from the sea, and noticing its lack of fear at my presence (though I remained still enough to placate it), I felt like doffing my cap! Here was one of the auks, birds of cold northern waters. Tystie is related to the razorbill, puffin and common guillemot but is far more individualistic. It has an abhorrence of crowds.

One writer unkindly referred to it as "pot-bellied inelegant". I prefer the assessment of E.A. Armstrong; in *Bird of the Grey Wind* he described the bird as a playboy of the western world. The soft, lightly-toned winter plumage of the black guillemot (so different in appearance from that of the nesting season) impelled Manxmen to call it 'sea-pigeon', and whalers — who met it towards the north of its vast range — dubbed it 'Greenland dove' for the same reason. The dumpiness of the bird made the strongest impression on those who saw if off Ulster, where it was called 'Tom puddin'. Edmund Selous wrote of "these little dumpling birds".

Black guillemots bobbed into view at many points during my stay by the western sea. Nowhere was there a large congregation of the birds. And always, once I had my eye educated to seeing them, did I liken them to fishermen's buoys. The brownish-black plumage was relieved by bold wing patches, a pied effect that was strong against the sea's brightness. Tysties were rather harder to locate when they had clambered from the water, to recline on their bellies soaking up the sunshine while staying at the very edge of the sea.

Coastal shallows are the hunting areas of the black guillemots. They collect food from near the sea bed. Fish, crabs even weed, are items on their menu, being taken

One of the brochs in Glenbeg

Waterfall in Glenbeg

Salmon enclosures in Loch Ailort

Thatched barn at Ardaneaskan

(above left) A great black-backed gull about to incubate its eggs

(above right) Great black-backed gull chick, newly hatched

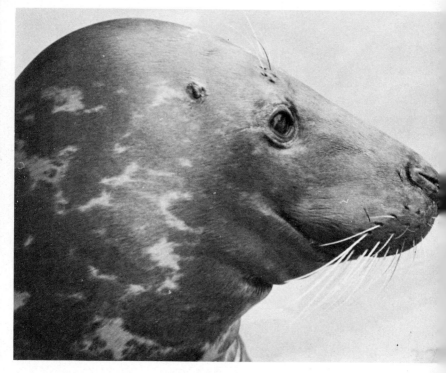

The Atlantic or grey seal

at depths up to twenty-five feet. This is not, however, the limit of their diving ability. Summer seas are bright and benevolent, but the tystie tends to be a stay-at-home. Many do not follow other auks southwards when the nesting season is over. Wintering amid snow and ice — and looking considerably whiter when in their winter plumage — the black guillemots descend in the dark sea for nourishing items.

By February, the nuptial plumage has been donned. Breeding birds assemble off the rocky stretches of coastline where nesting sites may be found. Tystie does not rush headlong into nesting. It may not be before the end of April that birds are clambering ashore seeking the nooks and crannies in which the eggs can be laid; no nest as such is constructed.

Meanwhile, the period of courtship is long, at times tender, at times lively and playful. It is undertaken communally, and the amorous birds appear to be dancing. The tystie whistles shrilly while swimming round another. Chases develop — above, on or even under the sea.

At nesting time, the differences between the black guillemot and the common guillemot are most apparent. Common guillemots pack a cliff ledge or the summit of an off-shore rock, being unashamedly gregarious. A bird deposits a single egg on bare rock, using no nesting material. When common guillemots are panicked, scores of eggs may tumble from the edges to be smashed on the lower rocks, or to fall into the sea. The species undoubtedly benefits from the fact that the large egg, being shaped like an old-time spinning top (with one end ending towards a point), revolves when disturbed. Fortunately many have space in which to do this.

The smaller, dumpier black guillemot deposits two eggs snugly in a hole. These eggs are pale, needing no cryptic pattern. Being roundish-oval in form, they cannot roll far. The tystie, nesting apart from the heady clangour of a common guillemot colony, hears little more than the smacking of the sea against rock. Incubation takes place at the end of May and into June. The protracted duty is shared by both parents.

The young of black guillemots are clad in dark down and
remain in the nest for some five weeks. Morning sees the peak
of feeding activity, with the adults flying in with fish that are
sometimes held crossways between the mandibles or may
simply be grasped by the tail. In due course, the food supply i
discontinued; the youngsters are left to their own devices. So
rich has been the feeding they have acquired a layer of fat, and
on this they can subsist in the short-term. The fat also stand
the youngsters in good stead after they have gone to the sea
Of two eggs laid, only one chick may be reared. It emerge
from the nesting cranny for the last time at day's end and
paddles away from land.

The black guillemot I watched in Loch Ailort eventuall
became uneasy at my presence. At a range of about thirt
yards, it performed an aquatic version of the ostrich's head
burying trick, half submerging its head. With the water clea
and calm, it would also be able to survey the bed of the loch.

Then the tystie slipped under water. Just before tota
immersion, the body was inclined forward and into full viev
once came the bird's bright red legs, which are powerfu
paddles on the surface and help with propulsion under water
If the tystie had surfaced with a fish in its pointed black beak
I might have seen the bright red of the gape.

The dumpy little guillemot swam around in a small area c
the loch, periodically dipping its head underwater. When
flew off, it scuttered on the water before rising clear, the
hurtled off at no great height. The pied effect of the plumag
with the bird in flight reminded a Victorian naturalist of
butterfly.

10

DESTINATION RHUM

We stood, the fisherman and I, scanning the raggle-taggle of Mallaig harbour — boats and gear, workaday buildings, men in yellow oilskins, fish lorries breathing blue exhaust fumes into the morning air, and herring gulls perched at six-inch intervals along the jetty railings.

Gulls thatched with their feathers the rocks immediately outside the harbour. It was raining, and beads of moisture dripped from the end of the gulls' yellow, red-spotted beaks. It was siesta time. The working shifts of the gulls were related to the arrival of the fishing boats and the unloading of the catch; to the periods just before fish wagons were driven hard along the winding road to Fort William, then far beyond.

Every Mallaig day begins with a round of gull calls. Each bird's maniacal laughter contributes to a medley which has an ear-splitting intensity. I saw herring gulls, the species of home waters. When a herring gull is not filching from the fish boxes, or scavenging on the shore, it attends the local tips, living off the discarded food scraps of an affluent society.

A regular source of food at the tips has encouraged the lesser black-backed gull to dawdle in Britain when the nesting season is over, though many still follow a traditional migration route southwards to the Iberian peninsula, even to North Africa.

The voice of a great black-backed gull sounded irritably — a bass voice among baritones.

Mallaig is strictly utilitarian, designed with work in mind. It is not beautiful in the accepted sense, lacking prettiness, but it makes a strong visual appeal. Many of the houses are neatly grouped in rows; they might have been put together from a construction kit. The white terraces of Mallaig were to be visible from points on Rhum, fifteen and more miles away, and can doubtless be seen even further away. They resembled rows of white matchboxes.

At Mallaig a thousand people are connected with fishing, in one way or another. They work hard. In 1965, I heard, the value of the fish catch was almost £600,000. Mallaig is not only a port for craft that stay around the Hebridean fishing grounds; it also sends quite large vessels on daily missions bearing passengers and cargo, and in summer provides a haven for holiday craft. At this time of year the white buildings of Mallaig are set in frames of luxuriant green vegetation.

Mallaig developed as a railhead, looking seaward, over the Sound of Sleat to the turreted hills of Skye. Pre-railway travellers used a coach that, bouncing along a rutted road, took seven and a half hours to connect Arisaig with Fort William. The railway still plays a game of hide and seek with the road.

At first, the Iron Road to the Isles terminated at Fort William. A port was needed, and Loch Nevis was considered but there were problems connected with topography. So the decision was taken to develop remote and lightly-populated Mallaig. Donald McDonald, a critic of the plan, declared "Mallaig is no harbour at all. It is just a pretty wee bay."

The West Highland Railway (Mallaig Extension) Act was passed in 1894. Viaducts and other large works were built of concrete because local stone was considered unsuitable. For the bridges, standard spans of fifty feet were used. Twenty-one such spans were needed at Glenfinnan. Concrete, in blocks, was also used for harbour work at Mallaig.

In due course, fish lifted from the sea, salted and packed into boxes, were put on wagons that clattered directly to the London terminus of King's Cross, the smell of fish combining with that of soot to produce the most distinctive railway aroma. For a human, the return fare from Mallaig to London was 60s.6d. — good value, the distance travelled being 1,202 miles.

On the day of my visit, the Sound dividing Mallaig from the Small Isles was a sombre corrugation of grey and silver. Waves began to grow white tops as the sea roughened with the approach of a gale. Yet these were 'sheltered waters'. The Hebrides act as a massive breakwater. Waves merged distantly into mist. The sea was periodically subdued, flattened, by storms in which blue-black clouds trailed sheets of rain to the shore.

The Small Isles, lying south of Skye, are named Rhum, Canna, Eigg and Muck. About 200 people live here, over half of them being residents of Eigg, where can be found the priest and minister, doctor and registrar.

An island woman, with two hours in which to do her shopping, nonetheless gave me five minutes of her time and commented on local affairs. She spoke matter-of-factly, without trace of emotion. The weather, I heard, would get worse before it improved. She was a seasoned traveller with many tales of stormy crossings, including the day "they shut us in the saloon, it was that bad. They didna want us to see outside. Even the sailors were sick."

As she spoke, it appeared to me that islanders conduct their lives as if the islands were great ships, permanently moored, and the families are on continuous sea-watch. Do they refer to the house floor as 'deck' and a wall as 'bulkhead'? The islander is a compulsive radio listener, with the weather forecast given top priority. Local weather and sea-moods are known and respected. The day is punctuated by a consulation of the barometer. It is rapped with the urgent intensity of a great spotted woodpecker 'drumming' in spring.

I discovered that the folk heroes of Mallaig and the isles are the boatmen – they who take charge of a variety of craft, from a converted fishing boat to a majestic car ferry operated by MacBraynes. Someone nudged me and pointed to a skipper, observing, "Weather must be getting bad. He's put on his cap!" Each skipper is known by his daily foibles, talents, accomplishments and (very occasionally) his misjudgements. All the details are filed away in folk memory, to be brought out, retold so often the stories acquire a polish, and commented on in the evenings over 'wee drams'.

Most of the stories have an undertone of humour. People are inclined to laugh with relief when they are standing on firm ground and a gale is tormenting the sea. There are stories as heroic as the old Norse sagas. Verbal superfluity is absent. Like all good tales, a story about grim weather and a turbulent sea has a 'twist' at the end.

The woman at Mallaig told me of the time when she sat on a deck-seat and periodically retracted her legs as waves advanced along the planking. I heard of a wedding party that arrived at Mallaig from the Small Isles soaked to the skin. A 'wee boat', hours late according to the timetable, was glimpsed briefly as it overtopped an enormous wave in the mouth of a loch and then sank deeply from view in a trough. The skipper had made it, but "that day even the gulls were grounded".

The relief at coming ashore on wild days is considerable. Teeth chatter like castanets. Heavy clothes are twice as heavy as normal because they are saturated. Every joint in the body creaks. The mind has slipped into neutral. Whisky, 'water of life', is then taken as a medicine, for "ye canna manish wi'oot it".

Everyone praises the landladies of Mallaig. They are ready for any emergency, have abundant patience and yet regularly muster the considerable zest and enthusiasm needed to rouse guests at some ridiculously early hour and have them fed in time to catch a boat.

Islanders, unlike the bees, remember only the sunless hours. When the Hebrides are not storm-wracked, they rise colourfully above a blue sea. I recalled the Sound of Sleat when it was so calm the ship's wake took on a herringbone pattern and I could look beneath the surface of the water to where jellyfish moved serenely in full rig.

Storm stories are preferred by visitors. They hear whimsical tales of other sorts of weather — fog, for instance. A boat set off from Mallaig to one of the islands when visibility was just a few yards, and over twelve hours were spent out of sight of land. Such was the fog's density that the skipper did not know where he was. He just commanded "hard to port" and "hard to starboard" until darkness came and he was on the verge of prostration. Then (miraculously, his weary passengers claimed) he saw the lights of Mallaig harbour a few hundred yards away. If the tale is not true, it deserves to be!

On a day when the sea was rough and the air keen and damp, I walked stiff-limbed from the boat and sought warmth and comfort in a hotel at Mallaig, refusing to stir from the edge of the fireplace until I had thawed out. The waitress winced when I handed her a tip, for the coin I took from my pocket had been close to the coal fire and was quite hot!

Morning at Mallaig. I splashed my way through puddles to the jetty from which the boat would sail to the Small Isles. Would it be the small but seaworthy craft of Bruce Watts? Or one of the MacBrayne boats? I half-hoped it would be the former, but indeed the *Loch Arkaig* came into view. She fidgetted at the moorings as though anxious for her day's stint to begin.

MacBraynes became a power to be reckoned with in the Western Isles. It was said that

> the world belongs unto the Lord
> And all that it contains
> Except for all the Western Isles
> And they are The MacBraynes.

David MacBrayne, the founder, "made circumstances, sending his steamers into Scottish underdeveloped ports, and encouraging the crofter-fisherman to send his stirks, fish and produce to the markets of the South". There was mutual satisfaction. David managed, nicely, to balance his books at the end of the year!

Loch Arkaig is named after the fine freshwater loch that extends deep among the hills near Spean Bridge. The craft was launched during the 1939-45 War, as a mine-sweeper. I went aboard five minutes before the appointed time for sailing but about thirty-five minutes elapsed before the *Arkaig* actually sailed. One of the passengers needed special, prolonged attention. The other passengers stared with mild interest as an Aberdeen Angus bull in a blue wood container was swung aboard. It was a young beast, which would dearly have loved to kick its way to freedom, but the man who devised the container had known the ways of cattle. The bull could stand, comfortably enough; its blood circulation was unimpaired, but no room existed for it to protest at its imprisonment by kicking out. Later, on Rhum, I would see some Highland cattle that had been conveyed to the island by landing craft but, disliking the procedure as soon as they saw the boat, broke free and made off inland.

I switched my attention from the bull now being swung high by a crane before being deposited on the foredeck of the *Arkaig*. My concentration now focussed on the man standing next to me and, in particular, on a bulge, about the size and shape of a whisky bottle, in a side pocket of his raincoat. He confirmed that the bulge was whisky. He was going to a 'dry island — dry, that is, because there was no inn. My fellow passenger spoke about whisky in such a way that he clearly revered it.

There are, he asserted, forty-nine true malt whiskies, and hundreds of blends. "Beer is fattening. Whisky stimulates the heart. It tunes up the 'system'," he said. Whisky also kept out the cold. "It's best drunk neat, but you're allowed a wee drop o' water — nothing else."

I heard of a Highland inn where so many empty whisky bottles lay around that the landlord decided to make them into a wall, heaping them up and cementing them together. The wall was impressive, decorative — and unique. One windy night, the blast whistled and wailed among the bottle necks. Next day the landlord had to plug them!

"Whisky", wrote William Larkin in 1818, "is to be full as much a staple commodity as black cattle, sheep and wool . . . and the smuggling of whisky is the only resource fo the regular payment of rents. The heavy duties on home-made spirits having debased the quality while it has raised the price, the superiority of the smuggled article is so palpable that the demand for it is universal."

It was now convenient to switch the topic — from whisky to Rhum! Was Rum a 'wet' island and was the 'h' added to sober up the name? In fact, the name — which is still variously spelt Rhum and Rum — could be pre-Celtic, referring to the island's shape, that of a lozenge. This lozenge is eight miles across! In the realm of fancy is Hugh Miller's assertion (1845) that Rhum's hills are "packed so closely squarely together, like rum-bottles in a case-basket".

The *Arkaig*, now ready for sea, trembled as the power of the engines increased. I watched a cormorant floating low in the water, only twenty yards from the boat. Was it looking for discarded fish? A shallow harbour like that at Mallaig otherwise offers no real challenge to a bird that has been known to dive for food at over 100 feet. Apparently the cormorant does not use its wings when under water.

The attentive cormorant cruised with its head held high but inclined backwards, so that the stout bill pointed towards the clouds. Do Highlanders still lick their lips when they see a cormorant? An old lady, recalling wartime austerity, said she often dined on cormorant to augment the ration. Catching a cormorant was not very difficult from a boat, and the bird should be skinned immediately to remove a layer of fat that might taint the flesh. Cormorants have a dark flesh and must be 'hung' for a few days before being boiled.

A former trade between the Hebrides and London shops concerned 'Hebridean chickens' — dressed fowl that were greatly appreciated by diners until it was discovered they were eating cormorant! Was this yet another fanciful tale?

Loch Arkaig, its links with the jetty disconnected, turned into a flow-tide, which smacked its white lips against a glossy black hull.

11

SMALL ISLES

We crossed the Sound of Sleat in worsening weather. Three
razorbills zoomed by, working their wings furiously and
having the assistance of a following wind. A cormorant flew
high and at a speed that looked unduly high for a bird of this
species. Coming from the same direction as the razorbills, it
also had the blustery wind at its tail.

The sea was sloppy and fretful. Single guillemots, or groups
of about half a dozen birds, took evasive action according to
the whim of the moment. Birds dived, resurfaced, then
paddled furiously away. One guillemot used the crest of a
wave as a take-off point.

Arctic terns went by. To anyone with little knowledge of
birds, their creaky calls might have given the impression that
the joints of their slender white wings needed oiling. It is never
winter in the world of the graceful 'sea swallow'. When the
summer wanes in northern lattitudes the birds go deep south
to enjoy long days near the icebergs of Antarctica.

The sea was temporarily devoid of bird life. I went below for
a coffee. and the rough conditions produced a storm in every
cup. A member of the crew was preparing the crew's main
meal, of braised steak and onions. He worked with pride and
care, as though failure to satisfy his fellows would result in his
being tossed overboard.

When the cook had slowly covered the pie with silver foil, he
remarked, "This pie'll be all right unless it's rough when we
leave Muck. Then — ten to one — it'll come flying out of the
oven!"

The island of Eigg took a definite, solid form in the mist. The Gaelic name is Eilean Eige, 'isle of the notch', referring to a central V-shaped glen. The shape of the island when viewed from the air is something like that of a kidney. John Macculloch (1819) called it Eigg from 'eg', which he said is Danish for 'edge'. This reference is to the island's most stupendous feature — the Sgurr or Scuir. Rearing upwards like an immense mane, striated vertically, and capped at 900 feet by a block of pitchstone lava, the Sgurr might have been towed here from Nevada.

We hove to and awaited the approach of the ferry boat. This craft had been cruising nearby and now it bobbed towards us, breathing exhaust fumes. I reflected on the special sort of dedication to duty shown by the island ferryman — he who operates a service to the big boats in the local absence of a suitable jetty. Most holidaymakers watch the ferrymen at work on summer days and are but dimly aware of the conditions on a dark winter day, with a strong wind making the window panes rattle and stirring up the sea. Then the ferryman is pelted by rain or sleet; he handles frozen tackle, and takes up station in a choppy sea so that the big boat will not be held up on its island rounds.

The stay at Eigg was protracted. It was here that the bull in its large blue container had to be transferred from *Arkaig* to the ferry, and from thence to the lush grazings of the island. The container was swung out by crane and set gently into place. Some white froth had accumulated around the bull's mouth, suggesting it had been seasick — though a veterinary surgeon I met later told me that ruminants are incapable of being sick!

Only the ubiquitous gulls were flying. Visitors to Eigg until 1879 commented on the presence of the white-tailed eagle, largest and most majestic of the British birds of prey, a species that once was commoner in parts of Scotland than the golden eagle. Harried by man (and particularly by those with interests in livestock, which the eagles were accused of attacking), the white-tails lingered on in Britain until about

the 1914-18 War. An attempt to reintroduce the white-tailed
eagle was recently made at Fair Isle.

While scanning the sea for auks, I located two black
guillemots. Puffins nest on Eigg. The birds are drab in winter
but return to the nesting areas with the nuptial finery upon
them and with bills adorned by horny sheaths that are
coloured red, blue and yellow.

It was a land bird that provided me with the most interest.
A cock chaffinch alighted on the *Arkaig*. It came down to settle
on a rail only six feet from where I stood. I fancied that the
bird was bemused by its surroundings. After bracing itself
against the wind, then staring left and right, it departed for
Eigg. The tiny form could be seen moving about fifty feet
above a restless sea.

A passenger mentioned a robin that entered houses on
Rhum and was considered to be a nuisance by one
householder. She captured the robin and took it with her on
her next expedition to the mainland. In the event, the robin
was released as the boat lay off Eigg. Returning to Rhum
many hours later, the housewife was greeted by the robin.

As we approached Eigg, the shape of the island made a
number of dramatic changes. The profile was seen to have
altered yet again as we beheld it during the short voyage to
Muck. What had apperaed to be a volcanic cone now
resembled a long grey mane, or perhaps the dorsal fin of a
great sea mammal. Macculloch wrote in 1819: "Viewed in on
direction, it presents a long irregular wall crowning the
summit of the highest hill, while in another it resembles
huge tower . . . The height of the rock is sufficient in this
stormy country frequently to arrest the passage of the clouds
so as to be further productive of the most brilliant effects in
landscape."

A passenger from Eigg to Rhum was a missionary of the
Church of Scotland serving the Small Isles. He planned to
take a service, stay overnight at a local home, and return to
Eigg the following day. His congregation would consist of the
employees, or families of employees, of the Nature
Conservancy.

At the time of the Reformation, when there were fifty-eight families in residence on Rhum, they remained true to the Old Faith, even though the laird — a Maclean — had become a Protestant. The islanders could take this stand because the laird's sister also clung to the old ways, and it was assumed that Maclean would defer to her wishes. Yet one Sunday, as the islanders went to Mass, with their patroness at the head of the congregation, Maclean met them with a yellow stick, presumably a cane, struck one of the men. The people were driven to the new kirk, "from which [noted Dr Johnson, the recorder of the story] they have never since departed".

Muck, smallest of the island group, seemed to have had a struggle to remain clear of the water. Low, fringed by rocks, it is a mere three miles long. Muck is, however, a basaltic island, with good soil to add to the benefits of a mild climate. Potatoes are being lifted here, for sale on the mainland, before the end of May. The name Muck is said to be an Anglicised version of a Gaelic name for 'sea pig'. A passenger with whom I chatted strung together the names of the Small Isles and they formed a sentence: "Rhum canna call (coll) eigg muck!"

The *Arkaig* lay off Muck to await the ferryboat, which pushed its way through a dark, choppy sea. Beyond Muck was a grey-blue world in which there was no direct sunlight — just seepage of bright light from the edges of the clouds. A few seals basked on a reef lying between Muck and Eigg.

Sky, sea, rocks: all were dull, leaden. The sombre clouds did part from time to time, and then shafts of light touched the water, which they appeared to plate with silver.

Rhum vied with Eigg for attention. I saw the largest of the Small Isle group, composed of igneous heaps rising into impressive domed shapes. Five of the hills of Rhum are over 2,000 feet in height. Three of them overtop the 2,500-feet contour.

The island was born with a flaring of volcanoes in Tertiary times. Rhum was a centre of eruption. (Now the *Arkaig* was voyaging through curtains of rain and it was hard to picture Rhum's baptism of fire.) Volcanic activity was also strong at St Kilda, Skye, Ardnamurchan, Mull, Arran and doubtless some other places now covered by the sea.

During the Ice Ages, the ponderous Rhum, though born in fire, lava and dust, was large and lofty enough to have its own system of glaciers. In recent years, owned by the Bullough family, Rhum was a secret island. Visitors to this kingdom within a kingdom were not encouraged. The Nature Conservancy acquired it in 1957 and uses it for wildlife research. Nature trails have been opened for the benefits of casual visitors. There is still on Rhum the atmosphere of a private estate. No hotels or lodging houses exist here. There is no inn. Official visitors stay at the red sandstone castle built by the Bulloughs.

Arkaig, entering the Sound of Rhum, entered trough between the waves. I watched the movement of part of *Arkaig* superstructure in relation to the deep corrugations of the channel. Down, down, down it leaned until the vessel seemed bent on joining the submarine service. Then the *Arkaig* shudderingly roused herself and made a special effort. Up, up, up she came, in a flurry of white water — to repeat the sequence moments later.

A fulmar dipped between waves, confidently using the uprushing wind and conserving muscle-power. When it seemed likely that the fulmar would be swamped by a wall of water, it rose a few yards; the crest of the wave surged on just beneath the bird.

Other, to me more interesting, petrels were in flight. Although the south-western sky had filled with cloud that streamed rain, a patch of brightly-lit sea shouted to be noticed. Against this patch of shimmering water flew a score of long-winged birds that were black above, white beneath. They skimmed the sea with a verve that was possibly even more impressive than that of the fulmar; they performed an aerial ballet — gliding on rigid wings, dipping low to be temporarily lost to sight in the troughs between waves, even slicing through the wave-caps with their wings, before soaring again.

In view was a party of Manx shearwaters, oceanic birds that

pend most of their sea lives buoyed up by air rising from the
waves. To a Manx shearwater, wingflapping is minimal. I
concentrated on one bird which showed its dark upperparts
and then, flying on a contrary tack, revealed the white of the
underparts.

Shearwaters live in part on shoaling fish; they alight on the
sea and dive, using both wings and feet for propulsion, to
catch their prey. They come to land, grudgingly, because no
bird has yet devised a way of nesting on the open sea
shearwaters have their nesting burrows on Rhum, Canna and
Eigg, though the last-named station has declined in
importance, having an infestation of rats. Fewer than fifty
pairs were noted here in 1964.

The Rhum colonies are unusual. In view across the Sound
were some of the high hills with domed tops where an
estimated 65,000 shearwaters have their burrows — right up
on the hilltops, generally above 2,000 feet. The colonies are
active until early autumn, when the shearwaters leave
European waters, many of them to cross the Atlantic and
winter off the coast of South America.

This is not a specially long journey for Manx shearwater.
During the period when one of a pair is incubating the egg, the
other goes for a day or two of food-hunting and recreation. For
very shearwater I saw dipping and soaring off the sea that
afternoon, there must have been thousands in distant waters.
The quest for food leads some of the Rhum birds, it is
believed, into the Bay of Biscay.

On a late evening cruise down the Sound of Rhum, I might
have seen an assembly of shearwaters — rafts of birds,
gathered for the changeover of nesting duties. When the short
summer night has arrived, shearwaters rise from the sea and
le inland to the mountaintops. Nocturnal activity has been
forced on the shearwater by predators, notably the big gulls.

Loch Arkaig held no interest for the 'mackerel cocks', which
a Welsh name for the Manx shearwater. And in due course I
turned from looking at the flickering groups of birds to survey
the soggy hills of Rhum. Mist was being wafted around the

peaks. The eastern side of Rhum is significantly wetter than i
the western side. Peaks tickle the clouds, which deposit rain
on the lee of them, so the average rainfall at the south-western
corner of the island is a mere fifty inches but it has risen to 12(
inches a year on high ground.

When the *Arkaig* was running with the waves, and the
pitching and rolling were over, I concentrated on a warship
clad in the light grey anonymity of Service paint. A thousand
years ago there might have been a Viking longboat here
clinker-built, high-powered, with mainsail striped vertically, i
could easily withstand these grey northern seas. Many such
craft must have passed between Rhum and Eigg, and surely
the Norsemen used the peaks as aids to navigation. The
named some of the hills of Rhum — Hallival, Askival
Barkeval, Ruinsival and Trollaval, the latter being of specia
interest to me.

Trolls, figments of Norse imagination, were small, hunch
backed, malicious creatures. Trolls moved about at night and
if daylight fell upon them, they were turned into pillars (
stone. Were the 'trolls' of Rhum in fact the shearwater
flickering and yodelling as they flew to the hilltops after dark?

A young grey seal regarded the *Arkaig* gravely during ou
approach to Loch Scresort, in which we were met by a thir
ferryboat. People and goods were transferred with little fuss.

The *Arkaig* moved regally off towards Canna, 'garden of th
Hebrides'. Here, at the farthest point west of the Small Isle.
the big boat would at last have a harbour in which t
recuperate from the sea's buffeting.

(above) View of Eigg and Rhum from near Mallaig

(below) The White Sands of Morar

(above left) Razorbill
(above right) Cormorant on its nest
(left) Kittiwakes

12

ISLAND DAYS

Rhum's ferryboat, stout and broad of beam, could cruise where the *Arkaig* feared to go. Loch Scresort, the only indentation of a reasonable size on the island's coastline, is quite shallow. Littering the sand and rock of the shoreline was weed, the 'tangle' of the isles. The ferryman told me that red deer, venturing from cover in the half light, trudge about the shore and nibble the weed.

I was, theoretically, at the lee of Rhum, but a plantation of young conifers on the northern shore of Scresort had suffered from the sea's ill-humour. The trees were dishevelled and brown, having been gale-tossed and drenched by salt spray. The jetty, alongside which the ferryboat ran, was slimy green with weed. The boatmen urged caution.

I did not feel to be on an island. There were hills around the loch. Northwards lay Torridonian terraces — sandstones and shales in conspicuously distinct beds, shifted from the horizontal by some ancient land disturbance. The impression was of a landscape capsizing, slowly slipping beneath the sea.

Scresort was at least sheltered from the south-westerly blasts. (The wind direction would shift, however, and a procession of storms would run down the big valley of which the loch appeared to be a water-filled section).

Rhum is a big island, running to nearly 30,000 acres. On it live only a score of people. What I missed, during my first few hours here, was an island flavour. Not until I had ascended one of the 2,000-foot hills would I see open water in every direction and confirm for myself Rhum's island status. Then Rhum would seem to amply meet the definition of an island in a Scottish report of 1861 — "any piece of solid land surrounded by water, which affords sufficient vegetation to support one or more sheep or which is inhabited by man". In Rhum's case, for sheep read 'deer'.

I strode ashore at Kinloch, the only inhabited settlement. A white-walled schoolhouse stood so near to the shore I could see the building's reflection in the loch. The names of eight children were on the register. I heard that the schoolteacher was the only resident of the island not employed by the Nature Conservancy or being a member of an employee's family.

A crumbling lime-kiln by the shore was being colonised by spleenwort. Lime was needed when the Bulloughs ordered the construction of a mansion — a castellated structure of red sandstone, this rock being brought in from Arran, in the Clyde. The stones were put in place by Lancashiremen. The Bulloughs, who made their 'brass' as Lancashire industrialists, clearly appreciated the work-capacity of men who were compatriots but not their social equals. It is said that the Lancashiremen were told to wear kilts, which must have been irritating, in two senses, each summer. To a dour lad from Lancashire, a kilt would seem ridiculous, and the midges would be able to fasten themselves to semi-bare legs!

The 'castle' lay out of sight — hidden by trees grown from saplings planted as 'bield' or shelter, and doubtless also to soften the austere appearance of Kinloch. Trees and shrubs endure because they are fenced off against deer. These, and the sheep formerly kept on Rhum, decimated the island vegetation by their browsing, preventing natural regeneration. Native trees and shrubs grow in places where animals cannot reach. This vegetation must be sought on cliffs and in some of the ravines. A blend of native species was planted on the slopes of the Torridonian hills, again with the precaution of fencing against deer. Coal, not wood, is used in the grates of the houses, and a year's supply of this fuel is delivered at one time by a puffer from the Clyde.

A Nature Conservancy vehicle that passed me did not carry a registration number — another reminder that Rhum is private. There is, in any case, only one road to follow. It goes westwards from Kinloch towards the centre of the island, where it divides into two, one branch going northwards to Kilmory, the other to Harris. Rhum, an island of boulder-strewn roads, must wear out vehicles long before their normal time. An islander told me of the joy of going on holiday — of hiring a car on the mainland and being able to travel for more than eight miles without having to turn back!

Those who ride or walk to Kilmory find that the main residents today are the red deer. Crofters improved the sward, which the red deer now keep short and lush by their continual grazing and droppings. Records of the crofters are few; the community was asked to leave to make way for sheep. Now even the sheep have gone . . . . At Kilmory you see what remains of St Mary's church. In a long-disused burial ground is a memorial erected by Murdo Matheson to the memory of five children, all of whom died from diphtheria between 7th and 9th September 1873. A seven-month-old baby died in the following April.

I was able to contrast this gravestone with the mausoleum of the Bulloughs. Built on some high ground at Harris, it takes the form of a Grecian temple. Sometimes spray from the wild Atlantic descends upon it.

Incidentally, the Bulloughs — not wanting their dirty linen to be washed in public — chose Kilmory as the site of the island laundry!

In the early evening the rasping call of a corncrake could be heard from one of the few fields — eleven acres in all — at Kinloch. This land yields cereals and hay for the dairy cattle that provide the islanders with fresh milk. Hay made in the meadows is available to sustain the Rhum ponies and the Highland cattle.

Hearing the corncrake, I stared hard at a dense matt of grasses. The vocalist did not show itself. A harsh "cres, cres" was repeated, from who knows where? I could not even get a line' on the bird by localising the source of its rasping voice.

That the corncrake can fly powerfully is indicated by the

length of its springtime migration from Africa. On touching down, however, the bird is reticent to show itself. Once I had a corncrake in the hand. A butcher's dog plucked the bird from a local meadow and brought it to its master. We set the corncrake down on the lawn of a garden. The bird, quickly rallying, streaked for a herbaceous border, where we looked for it without success. Next day the rasp of the corncrake was once again heard from the meadow.

I retained a memory of a delicately-toned bird that was pale buff above. The bill was short, the wings rounded. When I visited Ireland, every other pocket-sized field seemed to have a corncrake pair — and may still have, for all I know. Yet now the corncrake is scarce almost to the point of extinction in northern England, while remaining moderately common in parts of north-western Scotland.

A villager at Kinloch walked along a path one summer afternoon and saw a corncrake lead a brood of chicks ahead of her. Another villager related that corncrakes usually nest in dense vegetation near his home. He sometimes saw an adult bird walk around the end of his building and down the garden path. Once he attempted to complete the rearing of a corncrake chick that had become chilled and draggled through being hatched out in a period of continuous heavy rain.

On my first evening of residence at Rhum, I crossed the Kinloch river (which, incidentally, is used for spawning by salmon and sea trout). A hooded crow clasped a mussel in its powerful mandibles and if I had not appeared may have flown and dropped the shellfish on rocks. In the event, the bird flew off, still with the mussel.

A red stag, with a lusty growth of new horn, hung about a few hundred yards from the village as though waiting patiently for dusk. Though it went from my sight, it was only to stand in the nearest cover, from which I later saw it regarding me gravely. A red deer hind animated the woodland near the school. I disturbed a small group of females at last light, and they departed across the comparatively shallow Kinloch river.

The folk of Kinloch accept deer as part of the scene, to the extent that they no longer really notice them. But telegraph poles have been wrapped around with barbed wire so that deer will not be tempted to rub against them. Wise management keeps the deer stock at a level acceptable to the island's resources, and there are undoubtedly many more deer than was the case 200 years ago, when Pennant saw a few of the small native stock. By the end of the century, the red deer's association with Rhum had ended. The Marquis of Salisbury reintroduced deer for sport in the 1840s, and for a long time the deer had to co-exist with sheep. Most of Rhum's present stock of 1,500 red deer lie out on the hills and make a brisk retreat well ahead of any human intruders.

That evening, I watched a red-throated diver fishing Loch Scresort. The bird swam so low in the water it might have been water-logged, and then it submerged inconspicuously — slitheringly, indeed. The bird, from a pair nesting by a hill lochan, later took flight with the ponderous movements one associates with the swan and with a harsh "kak-kak". This bird, or another, was on the loch early next day. I saw it when, simply raising myself from my bed, I scanned the loch through the window!

Even before I sat up in bed, I had watched the passage of a cuckoo. Every islander has a cuckoo-clock in spring. A local cat stalked a cuckoo that perched on a fence. The disturbed bird flew from the side that was nearest to the cat and dipped in the air before climbing. The pouncing cat managed to collect one of the tail feathers!

When the summer gleam went from the sky with the onset of cloud from the Atlantic, I strode along woodland paths behind the castle, here to be entertained by blackcap and wood warbler, dunnock and the lively little siskin. Here, too, were the fenced-in quarters of red deer that had been selected for special study. I came under the stern gaze of a hummel, a stag without antlers.

The castle, its stonework a light red, looked bright even in generally dull conditions. The mansion of the Bulloughs had not been here long enough to have gathered much history.

Human associations with Rhum were already long established when the Bulloughs arrived in their private yacht and dreamed their grandiose dreams.

The MacLeans of Coll once had the voice of authority. (The family earned renown, if not widespread approval, by attacking the MacDonalds of Eigg and smoking some of them to death by lighting a fire outside the cave in which they had taken sanctuary.) At one time over 400 people worked the crofts of Rhum, but towards the end of the eighteenth century the owner of the island decided that they must go. It was more profitable to keep sheep. Many of the islanders emigrated to Newfoundland in 1828. When Hugh Miller visited Rhum in the *Betsy* in 1828 there remained one sheep farmer, his shepherds and 8,000 sheep. Miller wrote this sad commentary on the changes:

> I do not much like extermination carried out so thoroughly and on system; — it seems bad policy; and I have not succeeded in thinking any the better of it though assured by the economists that there are more than enough people in Scotland still. There are, I believe, more than enough in our workhouses — more than enough on our pauper rolls — more than enough muddled up, disreputable, useless, and unhappy, in their miasmatic valleys and typhoid courts of our large towns; but I have yet to learn how arguments for local depopulation are to be drawn from facts such as these.
>
> A brave and hardy people, favourably placed for the development of all that is excellent in human nature, form the glory and strength of a country; — a people sunk into an abyss of degradation and misery, and in which it is the whole tendency of external circumstances to sink them yet deeper, constitute its weakness and its shame; and I cannot quite see on what principle the ominous increase which is taking place among us in the worse class, is to form our solace or apology for the wholesale expatriation of the better.
>
> It did not seem as if the depopulation of Rum had tended much to anyone's advantage. The single sheep farmer who had occupied the holdings of so many had been unfortunate in his speculations, and had left the island; the proprietor, his landlord, seemed to have been as little fortunate as the tenant, for the island itself was in the market, and a report went current at the time that it was on the eve of being purchased by some wealthy Englishman, who purposed converting it into a deer forest.

That Englishman was the Marquis of Salisbury. A few families persisted at the village of Port nan Caranean, where farming and fishing were the routine, until (in 1861) the site of the village was deserted. Today it is occupied by wildlife. Red deer graze its sward, and eider ducks and gulls nest in and about the ruined buildings.

Rhum was purchased in 1887 by John Bullough. His son, Sir George, imposed on the island his personality, his whims and fancies. He made such a mark he cannot be forgotten for more than a few hours at a time. Sir George became a millionaire in the right period of our history. Taxation was low, there existed a large and cheap labour force, and rapid improvements were being made to domestic comfort for those who could afford them.

Kinloch Castle became a most comfortable island home, though Sir George and his family occupied it for a fairly short time each year. Built in about 1902, the castle was packed with fine furnishings and mementoes the Bulloughs collected in many parts of the world. Only the privileged few saw them. Others were forbidden to visit the island. Bullough visits were regular until the outbreak of the 1914-18 War, during which Sir George lost some of his enthusiasm for Rhum. He died in 1939. His widow sold the island and its properties to the Nature Conservancy in 1957, and they planned to restore a sheep-degraded habitat, to manage the deer at a population level the land could comfortably hold — in effect, to use Rhum as an outdoor laboratory. The study of red deer would be a primary interest. Problems discovered and investigated on Rhum would benefit land-users on the mainland.

I stayed at the castle with members of the British Deer Society. The building was splendidly, whole-heartedly Edwardian, right down to the style of the electrical fittings. I had an impression that Sir George Bullough had just gone for a stroll in the hills and would be back for dinner.

To catalogue the castle's features would be tedious. If its contents had been sold in a limited period, the antique market would surely have been depressed for years! I recall seeing a golden eagle of immense size. It was a statue, cast in bronze, which had a turret room to itself. The weight of this eagle had been estimated at three tons. Such was the craftmanship that every feather had every barb clearly defined.

There was, inevitably, a stuffed eagle, and also some eagle eggs. Mounting birds and beasts was a craze at the time Sir George took over at Rhum. A mountain hare that beheld me with glassy eyes had been slain and mounted in its coat of winter white. Mounted fish of tropical origin were stated to have been caught by Sir George and his wife. Her ladyship was drawing in one huge fish when it was attacked by a shark. It was nonetheless mounted — minus its tail!

In the balmy days before the First World War shattered the British social structure, the Bulloughs might cruise for months in the Far East, using their own steam yacht. The yacht *Rhum* (from another rendering of the island's name) bore them to the island for their holidays. This vessel is represented at the castle by pictures and mementoes. The estate boat used today has the same name.

The castle and its environs were immaculate. The former lawns have become meadows. Grass would be mown to be sun and wind-dried for hay. A gateway set in a 'gazebo' is kept closed to prevent entry by deer.

I looked into an outbuilding where venison is hung. Nearby in a railed-off plot, deer bones were strewn, here to be cleansed by insects prior to being studied. A few antlers testified to the fitness of Rhum stags, but most of the antlers had been left on the hill to be chewed up by the deer. Antlers contain calcium, which the stags need to assist the growth of new antlers and the hinds can use at a time when they are pregnant.

Sheep no longer range the hills of Rhum. Tough-looking but amiable Highland cattle now help to crop the vegetation. As I have already briefly noted, they arrived on Rhum from Mallaig by landing craft. Difficulties arose when the beast objected to being loaded on to the craft. Now I heard more details — of how four of the animals took fright, several

andlers were tossed and the cattle made off, to be eventually
racked down and anaesthetised by dart gun!

A group of Rhum ponies cropped a hillside near Kinloch.
The small troupe of ponies had a fair amount of liberty. Some
f them had long manes and tails the colour of straw. One
ooked at me through one eye, the other being obscured by the
lowing mane. I was reminded of a former idol of the cinema,
'eronica Lake!

The stock of ponies is said to have descended from animals
hat escaped from a wrecked galleon of the Spanish Armada.
t is an unlikely tale. Stories of this kind are told about other
oastal areas of Britain. A galleon must have been like Noah's
Ark, disgorging strange beasts on to our shores. There is, for
xample, a fanciful tale in the English Lake District that
Ierdwick sheep clambered ashore from a galleon wrecked off
t Bees Head.

The Rhum ponies, strong and sure-footed, are of a Western
sles type, which has been used for centuries, both as pack
nimals and under saddle. They stand no higher than
ourteen hands. Most of them, indeed, are from 13.1 to 13.3
ands high. These ponies come in several colours — mouse-
un (with a dark eel stripe along the back), chestnut (with
ilver mane), bay or black. The Nature Conservancy believes
hat the ponies originated from a cross between an Arab sire
nd a West Highland mare. Long 'heafed' to island grazings,
nd facing the special local conditions, the ponies are now
pecial to Rhum. So is a species of mouse.

The Rhum wren turns up everywhere, from seacoast to
illtop. Climbing one of the 2,500-footers, I stopped beside a
urn to rest. The tallest vegetation for a mile or so was rank
eather, yet a wren was present, foraging among the ling at
he edge of the water. In hill country, wrens have been known
o nest close to the golden eagle. A pair of Pennine wrens
igged their nest with feathers taken from the prey of a pair of
eregrine falcons, which were nesting close by!

One evening, the midges kept me indoors. Battalions of
idges rose from areas of wetland beyond the castle during

the day's muggy decline; the battalions formed into brigade and their single aim appeared to be to harass men an animals. A friend who spent a night or two at Kinloch cast! left the bedroom window open, and the light on. He returne to the room to find midges lying thickly everywhere. Before h could go to bed, a vacuum cleaner was brought in to speedil dispose of the accumulation of insects.

Midges love woollens. "Go out in a woollen jumper, and te minutes later it will be covered with midges." I heard tha some people put silk stockings over their heads to preven midges from alighting on their eyes or entering their nostri! Thunderstorms, which are reasonably common in summe are welcomed by the islanders, for storms offer relief fro sticky heat or flies. Red deer can go crazy with annoyanc when beset by insects.

"What other pests are about in summer?" I asked a islander. He muttered, "Tourists," but spoke in such a way h did not intend to be taken seriously.

13

SHEARWATER MOUNTAIN

robbed the mountain Askival, on Rhum, of a white feather
at has the power to invoke for me the spirit of a special
illtop — one that comes to life at dead of night, when the air
ickers with oceanic birds. The feather lay on peaty soil at the
trance to a burrow at an elevation of over 2,000 feet above
a level. I saw its flimsy white form while leaping from
ulder to boulder, trying to emulate one of the Rhum goats.
he feather became a prized souvenir of my West Highland
ummer.

It belonged to a Manx shearwater, a pigeon-sized bird with
thirty-inch wing-span. Shearwaters had been active off
hum when I approached the island. Now, on the 'turret' of
skival, I walked between the burrows in which shearwaters
ere nesting. And a grim, sterile place the hilltop appeared to
:.

Here were unstable boulder slopes, and patches of grass
at the red deer had cropped until they were as short and fine
sports ground turf. Swirling vapour is a semi-permanent
ature, for more often than not there is mist or cloud on
skival and its neighbours. Ravens, sacred birds to the old
orsemen — who named some of the peaks — call through
e mist with deep, dry voices.

By day, the highspots of Rhum may have about them such a
lm it would be an impertinence to talk loudly. Yet here, a
ile or two from the open sea, are the nesting places of about
,000 pairs of shearwaters, which are highly vocal in the
iddle of the night as birds flash in to the nesting areas. When
wn comes, the hilltops appear lifeless again . . .

My ascent of Askival began with a trudge across heathe
moor, with nothing to suggest that the sea was a mere quarte
of a mile away. From the first moment of that walk I ha
shearwaters in mind.

I contemplated a species that is two-tone, dark grey abov
and white beneath; that has a tubular bill and about its bod
a faint musty odour. The Manx shearwater was so name
because it was first closely studied on the Calf of Man. In fac
the species nests along the western seaboard of Europe, fror
Iceland to the Azores, but the colony on Rhum is somethin
special both with regard to its size and inland situatior
Islands off Wild Wales are noted for their shearwaters, and
'guesstimation' of the number breeding on Skokholm in 196
was 35,000 pairs.

The Manx shearwater is an unexhaustible traveller. Youn
birds have appeared in Brazilian waters a few weeks afte
leaving their nesting burrows on Britain's offshore islands,
fact established because light alloy rings were placed roun
their legs when they were nestlings. A Rhum shearwater, fre
for a day or two from incubation duties, goes blithely off to th
Bay of Biscay for small fishfood. The range and homin
abilities of the Manx shearwater have been ampl
demonstrated using birds from Skokholm. For instance,
shearwater released in Venice was back on its Welsh islan
thirteen days later. It almost certainly undertook the who
journey by sea.

This master bird of the air, that can move for long perioc
on rigid wings, needing to beat those wings only at intervals,
awkward on land. A bird that swoops confidently to withi
striking distance of the waves, only to soar effortlessly agai
has to nest in places from which it can scramble into the a
with minimum effort of its legs.

Vulnerable to predation by the great black-backed gul
other birds and rats, the shearwater has so ordered its life th:
the nesting colony is remotely situated, never to be visited
left in daylight. Each evening during the nesting seaso
thousands of shearwaters gather in the Sound of Rhum, ar

n the early hours of next day the birds rise and skim through
he air to the nesting burrows, giving yodelling cries. The
ncomers take over incubation duties or, if young are present,
eliver food. The night air is full of eerie shrieks and flickering
orms.

The path I followed to the top of Askival became steepish,
ut was nowhere difficult to follow. A local publication had
eferred to the climatic, vegetational and wildlife changes to
e experienced by anyone on such a journey. For every 1,000
ect I ascended, there would be a drop in temperature and
hanges in vegetation such as those to be found by travelling
00 miles northwards. "Beyond the dwarfed trees lie the high
rasslands and heaths and the barren, lichen-covered rocks.
bove these are the sterile quartzite slabs devoid of life."

The wilderness flavour appealed to Hugh Miller who came
o Rhum as a visitor in the first half of the nineteenth century.
le wrote that "the whole of the once-peopled interior remains
wilderness, without inhabitant — all the more lonely in its
spect from the circumstances that the solitary valleys, with
heir plough-furrowed patches, and their ruined heaps of
tone, open upon shores every whit as solitary as themselves,
nd that the wide untrodden sea stretches drearily around."

Miller, who strode in the evening, ran into midge problems.
The armies of the insect world" were "sporting in the light
y millions."

I stopped at a 'wee dam'. It was here, I had been told, that I
ight get my coughing done! The water was so clear that
very detail of the bed could be seen and stones that had
ttled in the dam gave to the water their lime-green hue. It
as 'braw' water, the sort to which a stalker had referred
hen he said, "Once ye start drinking, ye canna stop." The
vine down which the burn flowed looked like a jagged
ound on the face of the island.

I glanced backwards, along the path I had taken, seeing the
nocuous wetlands near the castle from which the midges
nerge as rampaging hordes on summer evenings. In view,
cross the sea, were the Cuillins of Skye. As I admired Skye's

turrets, was there a watcher on that island admiring, at t]
same time, a long view of the Cuillins of Rhum, from Barkev
to Sgurr nan Gillean?

The peaty ground of the lower hill had a coverlet of heathe
purple moorgrass, deer sedge and, in their thousands, t]
yellow, starlike flowers of tormentil. So it continued unti]
was over the lip of the corrie. Then grassland took over. Aw
to the west was the Green Hill, grassed to the top. Deer c;
thus graze all the way up its slopes.

I climbed to the desertland of the montane area, whe
poor, bare earth lay around boulders cleft by frost, and a fe
alpine flowers kept their heads down and developed long ro(
to reach moisture well below the surface — moisture th
needed when drought or dry and searing winds threatened
dehydrate them.

Mist came in from the Atlantic. A probing finger of vapo
ran over the high slopes, enveloping half a dozen red deer th
grazed a hillside. If I had not been looking at the advanci:
mist, I would probably have overlooked the deer. De
Munroe, writing charmingly in 1549, described Rhum
"ane forest of heigh mountains and abundance of little de}
in it".

From a ridgetop I surveyed the crown of Askival, which r(
like a miniature Matterhorn, composed of rock: shattered ro
and unstable screes. It was clear of mist, but gloomy becat
the sunlight had been cut out by the mist already pouring o\
its neighbour, Hallival.

Deer came back to mind when I found the first of t
shearwater burrows. Droppings from the birds had fertilis
the ground. The grass growth (which, incidentally, w
helping to stabilise the hillside) was finely grazed, and on
were deer droppings, and almost every burrow had wh
splashes at the entrance to tell of recent bird activity. Sor
burrows, as I have related, had cast white feathers in th
mouths.

Shearwaters are long-living birds. It may be that f
maturity is not reached until a bird is five years old.

ebruary and March the breeding stock assembles off the
esting areas. There is at first a reluctance to cross the
deline, but then nocturnal visits are paid to the old burrows,
hich are enlarged, cleaned and tidied for the season. In some
ses, new burrows are excavated. Individual shearwaters are
clined to return again and again to the burrows they used
efore, and courtship may take place within the burrows.

The eggs are laid in late April or early May, each female
roducing a single egg, the shell of which is dull-white. Eggs
und near the entrances to burrows early in the season must
ave been laid by birds which mistimed the moment for
ying.

An ordered routine develops over the fifty-two days of
cubation. Male and female take turns. One bird remains in
e burrow, and the other goes to sea for two or three days at a
ne. The shearwater's journey for food never ceases to
press us. Some birds fly beyond Land's End to the coasts of
ain, here to dine on shoals of small fish, sprats and
lchards. Fish are plucked from the water as the shearwater
vers over them; the bird may make a shallow dive.

The changeover in incubation duties occurs at night — a
rk night. Little activity is noticed when Askival is
oonlit. The summer night is short. Much has to be packed
to a few hours. While at sea, the shearwater is silent, but a
bble of sound develops around the upper slopes of the
ountain in the early hours. Calls echo from the hill.

A former warden at Rhum, Peter Wormell, pegged some of
e burrows. He cut away a section of turf above so that he
uld reach the birds within. Flat stones were placed under
e turf in order that the shearwaters would be protected from
splaced soil during inspections. Light alloy rings were
pped round the legs of the birds.

The shearwaters fly by night because then their main
emies, the big gulls, are roosting. Golden eagles prey on the
rds, either striking them at first light or when there is a
on. Shearwaters live partly on plankton; this and other sea
d has been polluted by man's waste chemicals. Eagles

living on shearwaters take in doses of the pollutants, leading t
sterility, abnormal nesting behaviour, even death.

A shearwater chick is brooded by a parent for maybe
week. Then it is left alone by day, but at night is provided wit
food. After ten weeks of gluttony, it weighs more than a
adult. The grey down of infancy is cast; the youngst
'feathers up', spending some time at night exercising its wing
at the mouth of the burrow. Deserted by its parents, th
juvenile fasts for a few days and is then impelled to reach th
sea.

The mortality rate is large, about 50 per cent. Rats mena
the burrows. Big gulls prey on any young shearwaters unwi
enough to be outside the burrows during the day. Disea
afflicts many birds, and others perish during the vital fir
journey to the sea. It has been known for young shearwaters
arrive at the village of Kinloch, where they have had to l
rescued from cats and, kept overnight by the friendly villager
have been released at Loch Scresort on the following day.

Lights at the village attract shearwaters. Peter Wormell ha
to discontinue an experiment with a mercury-vapour lamp
set up on the castle lawn. He intended to catch moths. On th
cloudy night over 100 shearwaters alighted round about th
lamp.

Looking eastwards from Askival, I saw a lochan
turquoise blue and, beyond the cliffs, a blue sea. The bulk
Askival had divided the mist into two streaming wraiths th
joined up over the sea, forming a grey proscenium arch. Fro
a knife-edged ridge linking Askival with Hallival, I watched
burn descend creamily into Glen Harris.

A ring ouzel called flutily, and I looked for the bir
Thoughts of the 'mountain throstle' evaporated when a gold
eagle swept into view. It was gliding a few feet from the ro
faces and passed some fifty yards beneath me. A raven h
been calling, as it does when it is harrying the big bird.

The eagle glided into a bank of mist. Its progress was sw
and soundless. For me, the novelty was of looking *down* on t
bird. Most views had been upwards, against the sky, with t

Castellated mansion of the Bullough family on the island of Rhum

(*left*) Highland cattle on Rhum

(*below*) Common guillemots a

agle darkly outlined against bright light.

The white-tailed eagle nested on Rhum, but the link etween the 'sea eagle' and the island was snapped in 1907, argely through the persecution of man. No one molests the olden eagles, which are in any case protected by the law. Rhum holds few red grouse and no hares (on which mainland agles frequently live). The island eagles have been known to luck young herring gulls from their nests at the coast and, as elated, to take Manx shearwaters.

Did the shepherds of Rhum use prey dumped at eagle nests o fill their larders, as happened in the district of Gairloch? Osgood Hanbury Mackenzie related that shepherds tethered he eaglets to a nest long after they could fly, "because until he young birds left the nest the parents never ceased to bring uantities of all sorts of game to feed them, quite half of which vent into the shepherd's larder". The shepherd's staple fare of orridge, potatoes and milk was thus augmented by fawns, ares, lambs and grouse.

In thickening mist, I began my return to Kinloch. The sea iar' was not just a nuisance; it was potentially dangerous. The hills of Rhum catch the worst of the Atlantic weather. In erce storms the hill slopes have been covered by spume lown in from the ocean.

In clear weather I might have lingered to see the red hills of kyc, which lies twelve miles away. Or, eastwards, have ocated Kintail's Five Sisters and Ardnamuchan Point. The veather was far from clear. A mist as dense as a dishcloth alled for exact compass work. I used a staircase formed of oose boulders, passing many shearwater burrows. There was me to marvel once again at the navigational skills of the birds ying to the hill in darkness, finding their own burrows and aking over the nesting duties from other birds which had not nown the full light of day for many hours and must now leave n darkness.

The whistle of a golden plover welcomed me back to the vorld-below-the-mist. Then the umpteenth rainstorm arrived. That evening I crossed the dour heartland of Rhum in torrential rain, determined to see Harris before leaving the island. Harris, at the south-western rim, overlooking the Atlantic, had grassland that looked biliously green in the humid conditions. Here were Highland cattle, a few with calves at foot. Some of the red deer sneaking guiltily away had been grazing on the flat land near the Grecian temple under the roof of which lay the remains of members of the Bullough family.

Sir George imported some goats to Rhum, where they joined up with the ancient stock seen and commented on by Pennant in 1772. The goats are fond of the Harris area, but they live apart — aloof, indeed — from other creatures. On the cliffs they can remain cool and be free from the summer torment of insect pests. Breezes direct from the Atlantic waft away the strong body odours of the billies. A friend claims that a wild goat always moves into the wind to avoid its own rancid smell!

The goats of Rhum compel attention because they do their best to avoid it. Theirs is a strangely isolated life. Nannies drop their kids in January and February. So nature provides a regular cull. If the weather turns nasty at that time — as well it might — not many kids will survive to crop the lush summer grasses. Wild goats, like the red deer, champ seaweed and leave their slots on the shore.

The Western Isles, a converted fishing boat, conveyed me from Rhum to the mainland. In the Sound of Rhum we took some moderate waves on the starboard beam.

Shearwaters were active. I watched a bird as it rose, turned on to its side (showing its white underparts) and then dived towards a deep trough between waves, rising again, with wings rigidly outstretched. The uplift came from wind zipping up from the side of a wave.

I heard that on the previous evening, *The Western Isles* was cruising off the south-east coast of Rhum at about 9 p.m., in a roughish sea, when it passed between two rafts of shearwaters. Several hundred birds were present. The birds rose and fell with the waves like two large dark patches of seaweed.

Herring gulls, our faithful attendants, were selective in the food they accepted on the return voyage. Potato peel from the galley was ignored. Orange peel did not interest them. The gulls did not 'taste and see' but descended towards some jettisoned scraps and hovered a few feet above them. The scraps were scrutinised before a decision was taken to accept or ignore.

Our craft had a following sea from Eigg. A black guillemot floated just off Mallaig. With bones creaking at the joints, I made for the nearest cafe. Holidaymakers in western Scotland have to be tough, even in summer!

14

THE RAINBIRDS

Old folk believe that the wail of a red-throated diver presages rain. A cynic might add, with regard to the West Highlands — where divers are relatively common — that when the bird is silent, rain is falling!

A diver's cry at its nesting loch in spring is not a beautiful sound, but it excites and fascinates me. "Mournful and eerie," was one description of the wail. "A long-drawn shriek," wrote another naturalist. "Like an outburst from someone in distress," noted a third.

The cry causes elation, not distress, to those who know and admire the redthroated diver and its cousin the blackthroat. It is a true wilderness sound, echoing over soggy moorland from the lochans where divers nest within a few yards of open water.

The rain-goose's strange aria seems to reverberate through a succession of solitudes, and a diver inhabits its nesting area with a fine disregard for cover. There is rarely enough vegetation behind which it can skulk. When the moor birds — greenshanks, perhaps — sound an alarm at approaching danger, the redthroat may fly, or partly submerge, to conceal its considerable bulk.

Some lochans used by nesting redthroats are so small they are woefully inadequate in food. This does not unduly worry the birds. The coast is rarely far away, and the divers commute. The sea is benevolent to hungry creatures that have the ability to dive deeply.

Redthroats nest on Rhum. One evening, seeing a pair cruising on a lochan, I envied them their well-oiled feathers or I stood in driving rain. As I looked across country, and lightly downwards, to the silvery gleam of water, it was just possible to discern the forms of the divers, though they had been drained of their colour by the murk and rain.

The grey forms were distinguishable as birds because they moved. They were identifiable as redthroats because of their size, the thickness of the necks and, more precisely, because the slender bills were uptilted. This jaunty angle of the peak — a redthroat characteristic — follows the acute angulation of the lower mandible. A friend claims that the redthroats is struggling against the effects of a collar that is too tight!

I squelched across the northern part of Rhum, looking at some of the many lochans where redthroats might breed. Afternoon is a languid time for wildlife, but a redthroat flew over, moving high. Mainland nesters have a choice from 0,000 lochans, many of which are infrequently visited by man. In Britain, the divers are at the southern end of a vast circumpolar range. Outside the nesting season, these rainbirds look paler, having moulted into a less striking winter plumage.

Winter views of the rainbirds tend to be indistinct and vague. The birds are not restricted, as at nesting time, to a small area. In good light, a bold silhouette may be seen against a sparkling sea. When the weather is poor, and rain and sea look to have blended in a study in greys, the diver is an insubstantial blob. A friend enjoys locating his divers far out because he has a telescope that resembles a six-inch gun; what are black dots to the naked eye resolve themselves through the lenses as definable birds.

A diver is plain — utilitarian, cigar-shaped, with no special adornments such as head plumes. The wings are comparatively small. You would imagine them insufficient to sustain the bird in flight — when, incidentally, they appear to be set well back. The webbed feet are so far back in flight they protrude beyond the tail.

I have already recalled watching redthroats while sitting up in bed on the island of Rhum. It remains a delectable memory. Early in the morning, with sunlight banding the Torridonian hills, and the loch calm, the redthroats down from the hills dived for food. A bird in flight has a distinctive hump-backed form; the descent to the sea is quite steep and, striking water with chest and belly, a bird holds up its wings for a while until the forward surge has abated — and the spray settled.

If the redthroat looks graceful on water, it is sublimely so under the surface, as can be seen on clear sunny days by those with the patience to sit quietly on the rocks overlooking little bays on the north-west coast. The progress of the divers can be followed to the bed of the sea.

The redthroated diver, commonest, smallest and liveliest of the three species of diver seen regularly in Britain, feeds habitually in salt water. Its nesting lochan therefore need not be large. Tundral pools are adequate for many birds nesting in the Arctic.

When seeking food, the redthroats of Scresort invariably sank effortlessly, without fuss or flurry. As they surfaced, with the forepart of their bodies so low in the water they were awash, I could take in points about their plumage. A redthroat has a blue-grey head and neck, with back and wings of ashy grey. The eye-catching feature, from which the bird's name was derived, is a rust-red patch at the throat.

A bird that swims with effortless ease, and dives with power and grace, moves awkwardly on land. Here it walks in a laboured way. Or it jerks itself forward on its breast which, during the course of the nesting season, becomes stained with peat. A prominent pathway is made as vegetation is crushed or displaced along the line taken by the diver from water's edge to the shallow depression in which eggs have been laid.

The scarcer black-throated diver, a dazzler among birds, could be seen swimming on larger stretches of water such as Loch Maree. Another blackthroat appeared on a twelve-mile stretch of water near the Great Glen. Yet a third pair was nesting on a large loch high among the hills.

The blackthroat tends to be a stay-at-home; it does not

commute as freely as the redthroat from the nesting loch to the sea. By choosing a big stretch of water it can take over a stock of fish sufficient to sustain it and the family.

The blackthroat is said to be larger than the redthroat; but such a difference is not noticeable in the field. In any case, I did not see the two species swimming near to each other, so I left the distinction of establishing comparative sizes to laboratory-bound scientists working with dead birds and tape measures.

The blackthroat is said to be more timid than the redthroat. My best view was of the bird on the twelve-mile loch, and I used the car as a mobile hide. When first seen, the bird was about thirty yards away, but soon it dived, to reappear twenty yards farther on. A series of shallow dives led it a considerable distance away. (The dive of one blackthroat was timed at two minutes, during which the bird swam underwater for an estimated quarter of a mile).

The blackthroat, like the redthroat, wails in a melancholy fashion at the nesting grounds. The sound is the first of the two to be heard. The blackthroat has usually hatched off its young by the time the redthroat is thinking of laying.

The great northern diver (common 'loon' of North America) outgrows and outcalls the others. It is far less common than the other species in a Scottish context. As a boy, I read Arthur Ransome's books of adventure in which young people were the heroes and heroines. In *Great Northern* was an account, in the form of fiction, of the first breeding of the great northern diver in Britain. A remote part of Scotland had been chosen by a pair.

Fiction became fact in recent times. I heard of the successful nesting of great northerns and resisted the temptation to inquire about details of time and place. Rare birds deserve to have their solitude respected. Rumour had it that one of the pair – or another great northern – paired up with a black-throated diver, to the disappointment of naturalists anxious to see the great northern establish itself as a regular breeding species.

I had already, that year, seen two great northern divers.

Standing beside Loch Ailort on a blustery May evening, I saw a solitary diver swimming eighty yards from the shore. Its main features were those of the rare great northern — with a ponderous black bill, shaped like a dagger, protruding from a large black head.

That bird was disinclined to fly. A great northern diver is capable of strong, direct flight, but stays on the water for as long as possible. Flight from the surface of a loch has a fumbling start until the whirring wings take the strain of carrying a body that looks as large as that of a goose. The second great northern I viewed was cruising off one of the Small Isles, in an area where it had frequently been seen for weeks.

Divers utter a variety of calls. The best-known is the strange wailing that gives the impression of someone in acute distress. Such a call accentuates the wilderness character of an area. Naturalists love to hear it. Elderly Highlanders hope that the bird is not heralding another period of rain!

15

LAND'S END

After the rain, sunshine. After grey skies, cumulous exploding across an expanse of Mediterranean blue. The hills glowed. Birds shook themselves dry, and gleamed. A sheen of silver came to the waxy leaves of rhododendrons massed near my hilortside lodging.

Low ground still coped with the climatic excesses of recent days. I walked squelchingly to the edge of a burn that was running bank high; when the water had fallen into a deep and shady pool it swirled and bubbled darkly, looking like vegetable soup, from the leaching of peat in high places. A passer-by remarked, "The wee burnie's doing a bit." Sandpipers which had been flirting their tails, as they stood nervously on the far bank, careered away upstream.

It was Sunday. The day was well-named. All wild creatures except the boistrous sandpipers were as quiet as the local people, who walked or drove their cars towards the church for Mass. The men's suits were black as raven feathers.

The Old Faith remains strong in the North-west, and religion is taken seriously. The man who commented on the state of the burn had said, "If I canna earn enough on six days, I might as well be in prison. They'd keep me for nothing here!"

To the anglers who rose from their beds late with tnumping cads and furred tongues, after the revels of the night before, Sunday was just another free day. Visitors often offend the natives without realising it. A devout Highlander visiting a large town or city must feel like Amos, who left a bare sheep-edge home district and was shaken to his austere foundations by metropolitan excesses.

On the weekend prior to my visit, and away to the north of Ailort, I saw a reveller stagger downstairs and profusely apologise to all the hotel staff. He could not recall the events of the ceilidh the night before. He may or may not have caused offence by his drunken behaviour. By apologising to everyone he played for safety!

I attended the first part of the ceilidh. A party of anglers were kept merry by 'wee drams' and the music provided by two local musicians. These were not professionals — just local lads, with a keen feeling for native strains. They had stamina too, and kept up the music-making, on fiddle and accordion, for hours on end.

There were few pauses. When a musician stopped to drain the contents of a pint pot, or to let a 'wee dram' burn its way into his throat, the other continued. The first resumed his contribution without fuss, nudging another burst of music into the tune being played by his friend.

The estate bailey, conviviality forced upon him, did his best to be light-hearted. I am sure he would much rather have been at home, toasting himself by his fire, chatting quietly to his wife. The bailey was still fussing around his guests after midnight as they tried, with varying success, to find their bedrooms. Next morning, early, he was back and ready to conduct the anglers to the loch.

The anglers scuttled their floating kidneys with coffee. They winced at the brightness of the morning as they emerged from their hotel to look around. They wobbled towards the boats and for the next few hours thought of nothing but sea trout.

A new road, going westwards from Ailort to Ardnamurchan, cuts against the grain of the country. To me Ardnamurchan will always be Land's End. It is not only the western termination of mainland Scotland but, to the chagrin of visitors from southern England, it extends twenty miles to the west of westernmost Cornwall.

A road cutting about fifty feet deep testified to the boldness of the new scheme. The newly-bared rock was raw with crisp edges. Now it resembled a section of a quarry, but

s character would soon be softened by Highland winds, rain
nd frost. To the ledges would be blown the seed of many
lants. The rain would also surely wash away a bold message
n Gaelic which I could not understand. It presumably
xpressed nationalist feelings. Such feelings are strong in the
'est, where 'Whitehall' is listed among the swear words.

The new road swept along the southern shore of Ailort,
evealing itself slowly, in idyllic stretches, like chapters in a
atisfying book. Near Kinlochmoidart, a herring gull hovered
ver the road and dropped a mussel on to a surface already
ttered by shells.

I had been warned about the mussel-eaters of Ailort. When
ne new road was cut out, hooded crows began to use a half-
nile stretch as a cracking ground for shells. They then
onsumed the fleshy shellfish. Hoodies had previously
ropped mussels on to the rocks of the islands. Discarded
nells began to lacerate the tyres of vehicles and, even worse,
ne crow's new habits were emulated by the herring gulls.
ow, it seemed, the crows had returned to their old ways of
ropping shells on the islets. The gulls continued to use the
oad. It was seriously suggested that roadmen should erect a
gn warning motorists of special hazards ahead. Within the
ed triangle of the sign there could be a silhouette of a
overing gull!

Half a mile beyond Mussel Alley, hoodies were having a
ory feast on the body of a sheep freshly slain by a car that had
ot stopped. A big lamb of the year hung about, demoralised,
uzzled by the inertness of mother's body. A hooded crow had
sed its pickaxe bill to break through the sheep's rib cage. (On
nother expedition I flushed ravens from a fresh sheep corpse
om which the intestines had been drawn. Far-spread, dried
y the wind, the intestines looked like grey ribbons).

At the broadening of Loch Ailort into the Sound of Arisaig,
ystercatchers could be seen feeding on a muddy part of the
each. The Small Isles were now in clear view, dulled by cloud
nadow into a silhouette that was something like a cut-out for
 tented settlement. Eigg and Rhum, foreshortened by

distance, were hybridised into a single, long island of appealing shape and uniform tone.

From the hill I beheld Loch Moidart and the ruined cast of Tirram, a former seat of the Clanranalds. I trudged at th sea's edge from Dorlin. A castle which looked fairly comple from a distance was now revealed as a shell; it was gutted b fire as long ago as 1715.

The district, sheltered from the open sea by guardian hill had an abundance of timber which did not bear the tell-ta brown marks signifying that salt spray had swept inland.

The overflow of Loch Shiel sped on its lively three-mi course to the sea. It must be one of the shortest watercours in Scotland to bear the name of 'river'. Salmon nudge the way along the Shiel to their spawning grounds. It has been s for an immeasurably long period. St Columba, on a visit t Ardnamurchan, watched monks net five fish and urged th men to cast the net again. They would then recover a huge fis that the Lord would provide for him. The men cast and, course, they landed a fish. When the monastery at Iona wa being repaired, oak from the vicinity of the river Shiel wa shipped to the island. Columba intervened with nature when timber boat was being storm-tossed. The gale gave way to gentle breeze.

A sixteen mile-long peninsula terminates wit Ardnamurchan, 'point of the ocean'. A road beginning in sheltered area abounding in trees ends near a flurry of nake rock washed by the Atlantic. Frank Fraser Darling, in h *West Highland Survey*, called the region "Peninsula". He linke Ardnamurchan with Arisaig and Moidart, Morvern an Ardgour. Of this region he wrote: "Peninsula is the mos fantastically awkward to traverse in the whole We Highlands, a fact which is reflected in the much reduce human population, which was 2,779 in 1951, less than tw thirds of what it was in 1911."

Ardnamurchan was settled by Norsemen. From the mists time emerged Clan MacIan, and Mingary Castle was the stronghold. From this fortress-on-a-promontory the cla

aders could keep their eyes on boat traffic using Loch Sunart
nd the Sound of Mull. The over-enterprising Campbells
ecame locally prominent in the seventeenth century, many
embers of this family being buried on the flat ground of
amas-nan-Gaeli, at the southern side of the peninsula. To
e south of Campbell territory lay Morven and the Macleans
nd, to the north, the Macdonalds of Moidart. They were
uried on St Finan's Isle, near the outflow of Loch Shiel.

What would the old clan leaders have thought of modern
aluations of their poor, remote acres and the buildings that
ould be reared upon them? A four-bedroomed house, and
venty-three acres of ground at Glenborrowdale, on the
rdnamurchan peninsula were sold in 1973 for £43,000.

Ardnamurchan, a world unto itself, has a pleasant air of
etachment, being about seven miles wide. There is, in places,
lunar sterility. A Pleistocene ice-sheet swept over the
eninsula, gouging the rock it bared.

I was not conscious of driving on a peninsula. Passing
len, I was aware only of the sea loch on my left and humpy
lls to the right. The hills blotted out three-quarters of the sky
that direction. The road, which was barely wide enough for
e vehicle, developed with a succession of sharp bends. At
ch of them I reached for the car horn, but I did not blow it.
local man had said, "If everyone blew the car horn at every
nd, there'd be a hell of a din!"

The road, clinging to the southern shoreline, and often high
ove it, was edged by birches. It was necessary to stop to take
the features of Loch Sunart, for to lose concentration with
gard to the road ahead for a second would have been rash.
I looked, with eyes half-closed because of the glare, to islets
unted by birds and seals. Behind me, where small glens
netrated the hills, and crags looked darkly down on a
shevelled, deer-thronged landscape, the fauna included
lden eagle and raven. Up there were remote lochs, tucked
ay from the sight of the world, on which red-throated divers
sted in peace — untroubled at least by man.

Parking farther on, I scanned more islets. There was Risga,

where the eider nests and the summer air flickers with t
wings of terns. As the tide ebbs, grey seals beach themselve
to rest and sunbathe.

Wherever I go in the Highlands, I am conscious th
someone has been that way before me. The spirit
St Columba broods over the peninsula. At Ardslignish, t
saint was asked to baptise a child, but no water could
found. Columba prayed; water gushed from a place whe
now lies a well, and naturally it was named after him.

The headland named Maclean's Nose forced the ro
upwards to about 600 feet. In this district was Ben Hia
(1,729 feet). I travelled ever-westwards, over rolling, sed
moors, passsing near a lochan that was ten shades bluer th
the sky. Four hooded crows rose from a sheep corp:
Wheatears flicked their feathers and called with a clatteri
sound like stones being knocked together.

At the crofting township of Kilchoan, I looked across
Mull. A deep notch in the distant hills was Glencoe. It w
unfair to Kilchoan to regard it lightly, but by now an acι
restlessness had swept over me. The Point of Ardnamurch
was near. My speed of travel rose.

The landscape had been austere. Now it had an alm
pastoral quality. There were clumps of native trees — sm
stuff, like hazel, scrub oak, all hazy green with leaf. Buildir
had roofs of red-painted corrugated iron.

Bein na Seilg, the most westerly peak standing at over 1,0
feet, looking benignly down. The most westerly mainla
farmhouse came into view, followed by the m
westerly mainland buzzard and cuckoo. Trees were l
behind. The surfaced road gave out. At 2 p.m., on foot
reached the lighthouse at Ardnamurchan Point. The sund
near the lighthouse kept natural time, one o'clock!

The Lighthouse was a stone column over 100 feet high. O
hundred and forty stone steps within led to the lamphou
The 'Ardnamurchan wink' can be seen in clear weather a
range of twenty miles. Perched on the final flourish of rock w
a foghorn, painted red. I had the impression, seeing and ι

:aring it, that Ardnamurchan was holding up an ear
umpet. The foghorn emits a bull-like roaring when the air is
ammy with vapour.

It was an effort to look south-westwards, for the sea
immered. In view was the Dutchman's Cap, the most
utherly of the basalt islets and skerries of the Treshnish
les. That way, too, lay Coll and Tiree.

Birdwise, there was little to see. Shearwaters were visible,
it afar off. A cormorant went by, close to the sea. I returned
ong the peninsula. A raven soared over a ridge, showing off
s wedge-like tail. Black cattle and their calves were jay-
alking. Once, years before, I was held up for a few minutes
hile one of the beef cattle of Ardnamurchan suckled its
ung on the roadway.

I reflected, with admiration, that a local man appointed to
e committee of a Scottish organisation went to all the
eetings, which were held at Perth, from this remote far-
estern area, whose road system must have followed the route
ken by the local toper.

Ardnamurchan has what is possibly the highest density of
ldcats in Britain. I refer to the native species of wildcat, not
e domestic pussy gone wild. It is always worth looking twice
'tabby' cats in this area. The wildcat is a hefty animal with
:ough resemblance to a tabby. It has, however, a blunt head,
ortish ears and a well-covered tail that is banded by black.

Wildcats move to the hilltops in summer. A walker may
counter one, by chance, as it sleeps at a cairn or in some
eltered spot. In winter, the wildcat operates on the middle
ound, and a farmer I met had watched one crossing a field
hind his house in broad daylight. "Are the local wildcats
ily wildcats?" I asked. He thought that a number showed
ns of cross-beeding. The old Highland strain had met the
mestic moggie.

Eastwards towards Loch Linnhe, on a golden evening, with
ndpipers trilling from the shore of Sunart. One bird gave its
rill three-note call of alarm while bobbing its tail up and
wn in agitation and then flew low over the water, where

wing-beating was interspersed with brief gliding. Th
downward-curving wings almost stroked the water. Where th
narrow road I followed was hemmed in by trees, a buzzar
floated about fifty yards above the car.

It was a warm evening, but a chill went through me when
saw a sign proclaiming the village of Strontian. The elemer
Strontium, which was isolated by Dr Charles Hope followir
visits to lead mines on the hills above the Argyllshire village,
associated in popular imagination with radio-active fallo
from pillars of smoke mushrooming high in the air. Dr Hope
work took place as long ago as 1790.

In the shallow bay, where rocks are tangled with golde
weed, a floating kirk was established, to be used for over thir
years. The story of this novel enterprise dates back to 184
when there was a split in the Scottish church. The folk
Strontian seceded from the established church, but the
landlord clung to the old order; he would not release any lar
on which the dissidents could erect a church of their own. Th
villagers took to the water, and their floating kirk w
dedicated for worship in the summer of 1846.

Loch Sunart, in its setting of round-shouldered hills, had
strong appeal for the Vikings, who named it Svend's Fjor
The grandeur was enhanced when I watched a golden eag
being pushed aloft by uprushing air. Far from being out
control, and going just where the wind directed, the great bir
trimmed its feathers to the air current and ascended in
straight line. It was truly golden. Normally, the name appli
to feathers about the head, but this evening the underpar
were flushed by ripening sunlight.

The Gaelic name was *iolaire dubh*, or black eagle — an effe
normally seen when the great bird is illuminated from abov
A Highland eagle looks fierce, but is shy with humans and
harried by ravens and crows. It is thus always worthwhi
looking into the sky when the "pruck" of a raven or th
honking of a crow (a sound like that made by an old mot
horn) is repeated several times.

Summer is a bountiful time for eagles which are, in a

Near the summit of Hallival, on the island of Rhum

The Dark Mile leading to Loch Arkaig

:ase, catholic in their food tastes. After being nestbound for
nine or ten weeks, the eaglets let the summer breezes carry
hem on exploratory trips. In due course, the old birds give
trong hints that the young should depart from the home area
ind find territories of their own.

Glen Tarbert led me to the shore of Linnhe, whose calm
waters were that evening disturbed as a common seal surfaced.
The seal was pale grey and, as far as I could tell, a loner,
doubtless laying fat through nourishing fish banquets. By the
end of August the larger grey seal would go to oceanic islands
ind the remoter parts of larger islands for the turbulence of
calving and mating. Thousands of grey seals roam the sea and
sea lochs off the west coast of Scotland, but summering parties
of seals are rarely large.

Fishermen tend to regard the grey seal as a competitor,
hough it feeds largely on rock fish. It occasionally damages
ishing nets. Larkin (1819) recorded the abundance of herring
n Loch Linnhe, adding that "the boat herring fishery
onstitutes a principal part of the occupation of a considerable
ortion of the population of Inverlochy".

The weather changed, quite suddenly. A cool breeze
trummed the hills and made patterns of disturbed water on
he loch. The sun was underswept by blue-black clouds. Ben
Jevis donned a bonnet of cloud. A summer storm developed,
with thunder, heavy rain and the appearance of rainbows that
oked vivid against a backdrop of hills. The short-lived
torm cleaned the atmosphere. I continued my journey
hrough a bright but dripping world.

When my circuit had been completed, the clarity of the
estern sky lured me to the coast. The main road to Mallaig
as now almost clear of traffic. Travelling through a deer-
aunted gloaming, I listened to some appropriate 'mood
nusic' by Ravel on the car radio.

The Hebridean sunset was not the finest I had seen, but I
avoured every moment of the sun's demise. The sea, slightly
uffled and backlit, had broken up into myriad horizontal
ashes — shadows on the wavelets.

The Small Isles and Skye stood out as bold tonal masses. Blues, greys and purples were represented in the colour scheme. The few clouds that had spread across the salmon-pink sky were inky, like dark fluid from an alarmed octopus.

Oystercatchers provided a chorus at the approach of night. As they called, the light values declined; the islands darkened to purple, then mauve. When the colour had drained from them, all that remained were plain dark silhouettes, like pieces of paper stuck on the horizon.

Across the water, the Hebridean night shift of wild creatures would soon begin. I thought of shearwaters, massing on the sea between Eigg and Rhum. When the night was truly dark, they would rise to fly with yodelling cries, seeking the hilltops. Here their mates and young awaited food . . .

16

JOURNEY BY ARKAIG

The Commando memorial near Spean Bridge commemorates many gallant men. No site could have been better chosen for the benefit of holiday-makers than this hillock beside a main road, with an undisturbed view of Ben Nevis, Britain's highest mountain. The Ben has a hunched appearance which belies its true elevation and its supremacy in the list of British highspots. Cloud frequently sweeps across the hill, robbing it of majesty.

Ben Nevis, so often regarded as just a backdrop, is not the most stimulating of hills to climb. Casual walkers slog wearily up the tourist track to what remains of an observatory. Others brave the scree slopes of Carn Mor Dearg. The toughest walkers atttempt to set their feet on three 4,000-foot peaks in a day. Their course takes in the summits of Ben Nevis, Carn Mor Dearg and Aonach Beag. A friend joined a party attempting the most severe — and, to me, most stupid — venture of them all, the ascent of Ben Nevis, Scafell Pike and Snowdon in twenty-four hours. He succeeded, but weeks went by before his nerves stopped jinkling! A namesake was one of those who have died on Ben Nevis through accidents in snow and ice.

Tourists were in full occupation when I stopped near the Commando memorial. The ground had been pounded to a concrete hardness. Cameras clicked. Crying children were just bribed with the promises of being provided with sweets and ice lollies. Elderly folk sat contentedly with the sun on their faces, their minds switched to neutral. Others beheld the memorial from bus seats, from which they had not strayed for hours on end.

It was time for me once again to quit the main touris
track, which is as well-defined as the main run of a brown har
in the meadows. Loch Arkaig beckoned. Tucked out of sigh
between hill ranges, its road a cul-de-sac, the loch feature
prominently on the map but scarcely anyone I met in th
Highlands had taken the trouble to visit it.

Arkaig first came to mind when I voyaged to Rhum, for th
big boat was named *Loch Arkaig*. The area had fascinated m
since childhood, when I first read the books of two pionee
wildlife photographers, Richard and Cherry Kearton. On ;
hot summer's day in 1896, the Keartons went to Arkaig witl
their primitive but effective photographic equipment. In day
when months of planning went into such expeditions, the
entered the Locheil country and photographed one o
Britain's remaining pairs of ospreys. Twenty years later
ospreys no longer flew over Arkaig or plucked substantial fisl
from the loch.

The ospreys located by the Keartons nested on a woode
islet. Their gargantuan nest, high on a tree, was studied fron
an adjacent island. Richard noted that the female osprey, "a
if afraid the hot sunshine would do harm", doused its egg
with water it allowed to drip from its wings."

Today, ospreys are uncommon but not rare. After bein
extinct as a breeding bird for several decades, the specie
returned to Britain of its own accord, presumably fron
Scandinavia, first to the valley of the Spey. The nest by Locl
Garten is world famous and the breeding progress of the bird
features in national news bulletins.

On my way to Loch Arkaig, I stopped to look back at th
Commando memorial, admiring the contribution soldier
made to the war effort. Yet there lingered at the back of m
mind a feeling of regret. While the commandoes were in th
district a forest fire broke out by Arkaig, gutting
considerable number of the venerable Scots pines that had fo
centuries adorned the forest of Loch Eil. Today, years afte
the conflagration, dead trunks stand tall, lean and grey, bein
themselves memorials to an unhappy incident.

A single-track road with passing places led to a crossing of the Caledonian Canal and on to the Dark Mile, where massed trees keep the road in continuous shade. The stretch was even darker in 1746 when Prince Charlie took cover from the soldiers who attempted to hunt him down. The old mansion of the Camerons of Locheil perished, and the castellated home of today was constructed between 1802 and 1837.

Of the old establishment, we remember the kitchen garden because it was frequently commented on, being "established there before such a thing was known in any other part of Scotland". Uncommon produce from the garden was set before the chief's guests at his seat at Achnacharry.

The Dark Mile, a pleasant respite from the summer heat, is not as densely wooded now as when it sheltered Charlie over 200 years ago. A waterfall thundered over mossy rocks. The outflow from Arkaig swirled darkly down an aisle between trees. Larkin, being shown the "river Arkeg" last century, speculated about the local watercourses, then wrote: "The river Lochy, flowing from its lake towards the south-west, along the level of the moor, receives in its short course of ten miles, first the river Arkeg from the west, and the Spean from the east, and then the Nevis from the east, close to the walls of Fort William, thus carrying to Loch Linne and the sea nearly the whole waters of Lochaber from a range of 530 square miles."

Larkin also heard that the territory of Locheil consisted "of vast mountains and extensive woodlands, pastured by numerous herds of cattle, sheep, goats, red and fallow deer, with a small strip of arable land on the margin of the lake". At the entrance into Locheil from the moor stood a village, 'consisting of a few straw or heath-thatched cottages, resembling an old highland farm *toun*, called *Corpach*, from its being a common halting station for those who were carrying dead bodies to Iona for interment".

My road, breaking from the cover of trees, began its thirteen-mile course to the head of Arkaig. Now there was no shelter from the sunlight; its effects were doubly painful when I scanned the loch. Here the sun's rays had disintegrated into uncountable shimmering fragments. To look at the water for long was to invite eyestrain.

Into view came the islets of Arkaig. One of them held the nest of an osprey in the time of Richard Kearton. Cormorants perch here to rest after food-hunting.

The road became a switchback. It was, needless to say, a single-width track. A driver had to keep to a certain course with little opportunity of driving on to a verge to avoid anything that appeared from the opposite direction. A sure indication of this constriction was the presence of grass at the road centre. Short, drummy sounds were heard when the wheels of the car passed over light wood structures which, flush with the road surface, were bridges over tiny burns.

Wilderness came right up to the road. Oak, birch and alder were the principal trees. Bracken rustled drily, and the fronds nearest to the road brushed the wheels of the car. The leaves of birches standing by the loch shimmered when teased by a light wind. Sandpipers tripped and trilled along the shoreline.

The road was interminable. Every mile appeared to be three miles. The road undulated with a soporific effect. I passed young conifer plantations. The hills across the loch run up to the watershed that divides Arkaig from the sea at Loch Nevis. The sea, out of sight and therefore out of mind, is a mere seven miles away.

Bird life is languid on hot afternoons in summer. I watched a pied wagtail hovering in a cloud of winged insects. A cock wheatear chacked and jerked its body as it stood on a hillside that was broken up by rocks. Against such a terrain, the wheatear is inconspicuous.

Loch Arkaig ended with a shallow bay edged by reed. A mute swan tugged at water plants. If I had been asked to write a list of birds I might see among these hills, the mute swan would not have been included. With a docile look and a natural grace, this familiar bird is usually associated with the lowlands.

House martins drove themselves into more clouds of insects

and the white rumps of the birds were conspicuous when the rest of them blended darkly with the shadowy hills. Swallows and martins nest wherever there are suitable buildings, even high on the hills. Pellets of mud are bonded together for the nests, and I still chuckle when recalling the martins that visited a builder's yard for their nesting material, selecting cement. With the addition of feathers, this gave them nests of reinforced concrete!

A three-note call — "tu, tu, tu" — pierced the summer silence. It was the alarm call of a greenbank. At least two greenshanks were present, and one of them fed at the water's edge where there would be abundant insects. The other bird flew. On the ground it had been grey, with long legs and a long bill curving up towards the tip. As the bird departed for the moor, white feathers formed a V shape.

The greenshank, typically a bird of the 'flow' country, at its best in Sutherland and Caithness, is thinly distributed across enormous tracts of the wildest country in Britain. Its company always uplifts an ornithologist's spirits. Finding a nest can be a long and frustrating experience. It is usually located near some prominent object, such as a fallen tree branch.

Sand-martins were nesting on a bank at the roadside, an unexpected situation, high above the loch, open to all the winds that blew and on a bank that was only a few feet high, being capped off by ling. Sand-martins twittered as they circled near the burrows that would now contain their young.

These martins would be spared the anguish of those nesting by rivers. I visit a colony set in a river bank composed of sand. In most years, when a summer spate raises the river level, the lowest of the burrows are flooded. Another colony known to me uses a sandpit. A friend captured some of the birds after attaching cardboard tubes and plastic bags to the entrances of several burrows, thus trapping emerging birds. The sand-martins were released when details had been taken of their weight and condition and when light alloy rings were slipped around their legs.

In the following spring, my friend visited an oasis north of the Sahara to watch and ring migrants. One evening there was a 'fall' of sand-martins, and among them was a bird ringed by him in the sandpit during the previous year!

Returning by Arkaig, I fought hard to stay awake, such was the lulling, roller-coaster effect of the undulating road. I became fully awake when, near the outflow of Arkaig, a black-throated diver appeared, and a buzzard edged its way around a wooded hill.

The shadows lengthened. The air chilled. It was approaching the time of day when red deer would be active. Local deer share the hill grazings with the sheep. Some stags are fed near the old home of the Camerons of Locheil, extra provisions being given to them until April, by which time most of the animals have taken themselves off to remoter areas.

A few stags return to the old feeding ground in the gloaming. There is nothing special for them to eat — but old habits are difficult to break.

17

WHISTLING DEER

the northern latitudes, the summer night is a brief interval
tween long days — unless a slow massing of cloud leads to a
emature dusk. On such an evening I sought the 'whistling
er', my name for the sika, a newcomer to the Highland
una. Its ancestors evolved on the Japanese archipelago.

When alarmed, a sika utters a high-pitched squeal that
ngs around the woods and, from a distance, is like a clear
histle. A stag's proclamation to the hinds during the rut is
zarre in a British context — three whistles, each call a
escent of sound, rising smoothly up the scale to trail sweetly
id smoothly away. The silence that follows seems more
tense because of the unexpected, loud outburst.

My chances of watching Japanese sika near Loch Ness were
t good, said local people who knew the animals were
esent but had been told they were shy recluses, lying up in
ick cover during the day and emerging timidly to feed in the
oaming. "Och, but ye're wastin' your time," said the
ndlady at my overnight quarters in Fort William.

Late in the evening, with the sky still overcast after a day of
ually showers, I looked for sika with a resolution
rengthened by verbal discouragement.

A low sun underlit the cloud masses. In a fantasy of form
id light, the main cloud tones were blue-grey, edged by deep
eam and shades of pink. The road from the Great Glen to
ka country made a devil-may-care approach to the hills.
hey were round-shouldered, heathery hills sporting clusters
rock and a few stunted trees. The road levelled out, then
pped to climb again between birch, alder and ash. The trees

appeared to be massed on steep hillsides, but they did n
have the stultifying effect created by conifers. Light ha
broken through to the ground in many places. Between th
trees the grass grew fine and lush, as on a lawn.

I wasted half an hour of valuable daylight in scanning th
woods. Surely if any creature of sikine size was moving on th
green carpet beneath the trees I would see it. Eventually
raised my binoculars to take in the upper part of the hil
beyond the highest trees, where a belt of grassland, no
banded by sunlight, extended to heather moor.

Several stags grazed here. They were dapper and dappled.
recognised instantly some of the main sikin
characteristics — prominent white caudal area, edged b
black, white patches on the hock — and reproved myself fc
neglecting the open ground.

I served my apprenticeship to sika-watching in a conife
forest, a retreat for a few old and weary stags with youn
entourages. Sightings of deer were rare enough to cause wil
excitement, for deer had only to walk a few paces to be i
dense cover. As a consolation, I studied sika signs an
droppings!

Gradually I came to terms with the sika. I could now go ou
with the assurance that I would, given time, see the deer b
exploiting their weaknesses. I moved silently into the wind
avoiding sudden movements and keeping my feet clear of th
twigs which fracture with a sound as intense as a gunshot.

Other sika, in a farming area, were conditioned to th
presence of tractors and machinery, which they saw dail
One day, when I had given up hope of closing with an old sta
that lay on a grassy bank with open field all around it,
farmer's son sportingly offered to drive me right up to th
beast, which he did, with engine roaring and amid clouds
exhaust fumes.

I stood in a hydraulically-operated scoop asking th
farmer's son for advice about photography; he cheerfull
agreed to lower the scoop until it rested firmly on the ground
The tractor engine must not be cut, but now the vibration wa

nimised. My prints would be sharp. The stag remained on
e dry bank. We approached closely, up to ten yards. The
ka surveyed us haughtily for a minute or two; then, objecting
our impudent action, it bounded to its feet, departing with
excitement indicated by a considerable flare of the white
ir at the rump.

So often did I visit one fine stag in its rutting territory that it
ng around, if I did not press it hard. Occasionally it
serted its authority by offering a threat gesture, lifting up its
ad until the antlers stroked its back. Then the beast
reshed vegetation with its antlers. One October evening it
ondered off with four feet of thistle lodged between them!

The stags grazing on the hill near Loch Ness were studied
ross a quarter of a mile of country. Sunlight illuminated
eir summer coats of dappled chestnut. A dark stripe
tended along the spine. The white caudal hair gleamed.

No other species of deer, not even the roe, has a caudal disc
such prominence. I have seen even sika calves flare their
fty rump hair when reacting to excitement. The white hairs
the adults are extended until they are like huge powder
iffs. A party of hinds, moving in line-ahead formation (each
iimal bouncing up and down as though on springs) gives an
pression of being ballet dancers!

The Nessside stags were growing new antlers behind velvet.
ka horn is simple, cleanly branched. An adult stag usually
rries eight points. The sika's headgear is potentially more
hal when used in combat than are red deer antlers. Each
kine tine has a lance-like point. A fresh dead stag I found
d been fighting with a challenger, which had sunk a tine
ep into its opponent's body, apparently rupturing the heart.

It will be recalled that when I first saw the Scottish stags
ey were just clear of the birch and alder. The beasts
lvanced up the high pasture, moving a few paces, then
king a few mouthfuls of grass. I saw that the hillside also
ld red deer which, moving at a greater speed than the sika,
egan to overtake the smaller animals.

Sika hinds — one of them with a calf — appeared to view. I

had not seen them break tree-cover. They were suddenly
view, clear of a group of birches. The sika stags were darkis
deep in the body, with burgeoning antlers giving their heads
ponderous appearance. These dainty hinds looked dainti
still as red deer lumbered by and indicated the size scale. Fi
sika stags went over the hill out of my sight. The hinds, a
some of the red deer, settled down earnestly to graze.

On the following evening, I climbed cautiously betwe
gnarled birches and in that sort of gloom I associate with c
cathedrals. I felt to be vandalising the slope, across which I l
a trail in tall and sappy grassland. A deer track came in
view; it extended along the hillside. On my guard now, I rat
my progress at inches to the minute, being ready at a
moment to 'freeze' to slip into the cover of a birch trunk.

A deer grazing in a dip only twenty yards away w
recognisably sika, though I saw little more than its bac
topped by the dorsal black stripe, edged by white flecks. Wi
its head down, the sika had a limited visibility — a matter o
few yards. It relied on the delicacy of its senses: on five-in
ears that not only pick up sound but, with both ears workir
together, can localise the source of that sound.

A deer's nose is another 'line of defence'. I sometimes s
deer licking their nostrils, presumably to improve still furth
their ability to detect scent. A stalker had suggested that
should consider scent as I might think of cigarette smoke. C
a still day, it rises; if there is a wind it extends along tl
ground, its height and extent depending on the wind
strength.

A birch tree gave me cover when the head of the stag wi
raised. This deer did not languidly scan the area, as might
human. Its posture was fixed for a few seconds, and the
another posture was assumed. This stag was potentially a
eight-pointer, an opinion based on likely prospects. As ye
antler growth was nowhere near complete.

As a 'big boy' the stag would have dropped the old antle
early in April. Blood would trickle from the top of the pedicle
those protruberances from the skull from which new antle

owth begins almost immediately the old horn is cast. From
e beam of the new antler extends the lowest of the
ranches', or tines, known as the 'brow'. There is a period
hen the growth of beam and brow are almost equal, giving
a effect, when seen in profile, of an anvil.

On grows the beam, putting out a second branch
erversely known in the sika as the trez) and eventually
elding the 'tops'. Then, with the antler growth complete, the
elvet' shrivels and comes away, leaving a gleaming antler
at soon takes on the brown hue that makes it decorative.
esin from trees, plus dirt of various kinds, creates this
npression. The antlers most admired by man are the dirtiest!

My sika stag, now in clear view, lowered its head to graze. It
as possibly seeking the newest growth, around the base of
e tall standing grasses. The stag was a member of a small
oup. Three other stags revealed themselves, and the party
oved along a well-used path only twenty yards from where I
ood in partial cover. The deer worked the edge of the hill on
a easy gradient, moving in line ahead. Their pace was slow,
id they frequently paused to crop vegetation. They were
azing, not browsing trees.

Summer grass is, of course, rich in protein. A short summer
ght is usually sufficient for the deer to take in all they need,
efore retiring to cover to chew the cud and think whatever
oughts enter deer heads. Yet in the lean days of February
id March, the sika would have to graze hard and long. I have
atched deer stripping bark from fallen branches and
ewing it — a dark variant of chewing gum.

The four stags went slowly by me. Then I was foiled by an
d enemy   the contrary wind. A light and variable breeze
ad been strumming the woods, having sprung up with the
ecline of the day. Standing by the birch I felt a cooling on the
ft side of my face, then a chilling of the back of my neck. My
ent was being carried obliquely up the slope. The leading
ag reached what I presumed was the area of polluted air, for
e animal became tense, statuesque.

Would there be a short, nasal squeal of alarm? Or,

perhaps, a series of querilous squeals? I had not actually be
seen. Such squeals can vary in strength and tonal quali
from birdy calls to something akin to gruff barks. No sou
came. There was just a rustle of grass as the stags withdre
following the line along which they approached. Long aft
the first of the stags had bounded over the skyline, the othe
looked down towards where I stood. The silhouettes of de
against the sky were toned a soft grey.

The last to go from my sight was the stag that had be
leading. For a time only the head and partly-grown antle
were visible. I stayed in cover, deciding that the deer shou
have a ten minutes' start. There was a possibility they mig
not go far. A startled sika tends to go off at such speed
applies its brakes in the next parish!

Curiosity impelled the big stag to return. A silhouette to
shape on the skyline, becoming larger and taller as the anim
reached the edge of the ridge. I saw the slender neck, stretche
upwards. The forepart of the stag's deep body became visibl
Eventually there was light to be seen between the deer's bod
and the ground. I noticed the comparatively short legs. Th
stag bounded from my sight for a second time. Thankfull
there was no wild squeal of alarm to mark its exit.

I moved up to the ridge, beyond which lay an expanse
grassland, unsuspected by anyone who remained on the roa
and saw only the hill slopes covered by trees. Many deer mu
have grazed this area, for the grass was short and, doubtles
sweet. A sweep of green extended up the hill to where the
was a clear demarcation between it and the tousled moor.

That grassland was broken up by runnels from which gre
rushes and a few small trees. The stags were absent. I can
under the scrutiny of a small party of hinds. The oldest hin
advanced, out of curiosity, and then unaccountably relaxed.
squeal was sounded, but the sound was short, half-hearted
I saw no stotting, no excited spread of caudal white, n
burning up of surplus nervous energy by exacting movements

A red hind, standing about 200 yards away, received a fain
whiff of my scent, judging by a sudden change in its manne

he head jerked upwards. The ears were extended rigidly,
d the body stiffened. Uneasy, the hind looked directly at the
ea where I stood. The animal bounded away, taking another
th it to sanctuary beyond the next hilltop.

It was dark when I returned to Fort Augustus. Before I
ew the curtains at the bedroom window, I switched off the
hts and stared into the night. There was enough light from
her houses to illuminate an area of rough ground.

Grazing 100 yards from where I stood was a demure roe
e!

18

WHEN CURLEWS CALL

A second or two after I saw a well-grown curlew chick
sharp-eyed parent sounded an alarm. The shrill outburst w
also a command to squat and stay still. The chick respond
without hesitation.

I was motoring near Loch Ness. The curlew fami
accustomed to passing traffic, acted normally until I appli
the brakes on seeing the podgy youngster on its feet, in t
open, doubtlessly looking for food.

Instant distress brought a transformation to the appearar
of the adult birds. Necks were extended. Momentarily, th
poses were statuesque. Then the long decurved mandib
opened and the warning was given. As the adults 'scramble
with loud voices, the youngster ran for a few paces and th
hugged the ground, where total immobility, and a nondescri
colouration, would under normal circumstances protect it.

The circumstances were not normal. Fiendish man, and I
box on wheels, had taken an unfair advantage of the bird
The earthbound young curlew may be lying inert in grass
long and lush enough almost to overtop it, but I had mark
with my mind the tuft of rushes near which the bird was last
view.

Leaving the car, I strode across the rough ground edgi
the moors. So intent was I to keep the patch of rushes under
fixed gaze that my entry into a marshy area came as
surprise. The mire was indicated when a series of squelch
attended the lifting of each booted foot.

Both parent curlews were in the air. One, bolder than
mate, flew near with ringing calls and, alighting about twen

ards away, ran in an agitated fashion. The bird took flight, with a noisy flurry of feathers and more angry shrieks of alarm.

A hooded crow incautiously crossed the area. A curlew dived upon it with a whoosh of displaced air and rousing "uch, uch, ucher". The intruder, apparently demoralised by the ferocity of the dive, took cover in a tree. Was the hoodie really demoralised? It would not have been the first time that this dark bird with a grey 'jumper' had been set upon by curlews. And crows, working together, can systematically clean up a curlew's clutch of eggs or any chicks that have just emerged from them.

Such is the degree of predation, it amazes me that any curlews grow to reach that moment when they take their first sustained flight and are independent of the ground. The curlew pair that circled me may have hatched four youngsters; it seemed that only one of them survived.

I found the singleton, which had snuggled betweeen tufts of rushes to 'freeze' in the hope that an absence of movement and its dowdy feathers would protect it from predators. The young bird faced downwards. Only the back of its head and top of its body were in view. I had to crouch to see the lead-grey bill and legs. The bill was short and straight; that of an adult bird is about five inches long, curved like a scimitar.

The chick stared at me unblinkingly. Not even when my shadow passed over did it show any inclination to move. The yells of the parents made the morning air shiver.

H.A. Gilbert classed the curlew of the Scottish hills among the heather dwellers" — birds that "have their summer home chiefly or entirely on the open hill among the heather and the rushes".

It is good to consider the birds and beasts with a scientific detachment, but curlews arouse in visitors to the Highlands such strong emotions they are apt to become dewy-eyed. An ailing R.L. Stevenson, exiled in Samoa, remembered the Scottish hills and the curlews that circled over them. Stevenson knew the curlew by the old North Country name of 'whaup'. He wrote:

Blows the wind today, and the sun and the rain are flying.
Blows the wind on the moors today and now,
Where about the graves of the martyrs the whaups are crying
My heart remembers how!

In another version, the "peewees" (lapwings) are crying.

Stevenson's evocative verse put the whaup in its setting. F
referred to the "vacant wine-red moor" and to "hills of shee
and the homes of the silent vanished races" where there a
"winds, austere and pure".

To a Highlander, the silvery call of the whaup is welcome
as a foretaste of spring, which is usually late among tl
hills — so late, indeed, that there can be a month's differen
in the nesting dates between curlew's nesting on low counti
and those on high ground. A whaup's whistling arous
nostalgia, sometimes even melancholia, in the exile.

Wild, clear curlew calls punctuate the Highland summ
until July, when families of birds drift to the lowlands, here
join with other parties into groups. At nesting time, howeve
curlews are thinly scattered about the moors. They anticipa
the dawn with their outbursts and give a sense of life to tl
dreamiest of dusks. Curlew calls sometimes ring out durir
the night. A rousing "pic, pic, pic" may indicate that a dog
a fox is prowling.

The well-grown young bird I located did not move of i
own accord even when I had turned it on its side to examine
So finely-developed is the instinct to 'freeze' that chicks st
inert, in whatever position they are placed. When the
composure is shattered, however, they run off, with pipir
calls. Then the anxiety of the adults reaches a higher peak.

It was distasteful to pick up a young bird that was so clo
to being able to fly. It had hatched out and was brooded in tl
soft, warm, dark space between the ground and the undersi
of a parent's body. Here it had recovered from the exertions
rapping on the inside of the shell with its special toot
eventually to shatter the shell and struggle forth, its dov
streaky with moisture. Here the chick 'dried off', to l
revealed with a soft coat of brownish-white, mottled wi
chestnut and blotches of warm brown.

Eventually, the down of infancy rubs from a chick's body as he feathers sprout. Wing-flapping brings strength to the muscles and, in due course, the hard blue quills in which the light feathers are first encased fall away. The curlew lacks the ability to fly until it is practically full-grown at about six weeks. Big, floppy youngsters dine on a variety of food in the summer-rich countryside.

If curlews remained silent at the nesting grounds, they would often be overlooked. Their shrill voices draw attention to themselves. A curlew is a large bird — the biggest of the European waders — and is lanky to the point of being rakish. Long legs, long neck, long neb, are distinguishing features of such prominence it cannot be easily confused with another species, except perhaps the rarer whimbrel. The downcurved mandibles are a key to identification. They show up clearly when the bird flies, even if it is merely a silhouette against a bright sky.

A curlew stalks, hunch-backed, across a tract of rough ground, with the neck retracted and the head appearing to rest directly on the body. The plumage, of streaky-brown, is drab overall. How such a large bird can conceal itself is remarkable, but I have almost passed by a sitting bird without being aware of its near presence.

A bird on the nest, when alarmed but not to the extent of slipping from the eggs to run a while before flying, snuggles down so well it has the semblance of a clump of wizened turf even at a range of a few yards. Only the darker feathers of the back are visible. The head rests on the ground; the long bill is concealed by vegetation.

The voice of the curlew, expressing itself in a variety of calls, draws attention to this largest of the wading family. A flight note, "quoi, quoi", is heard from birds of passage. Those birds may be at a considerable height, but the silvery notes descend with strength and clarity. At times of mist, betokening a thaw, flight calls come from high over hills and also over industrial towns. Less pleasant to hear are a curlew's grating calls of alarm. A bird with hard-set eggs or young comes close to vulgar swearing.

When Stevenson thought of a whaup's calling, he doubtle[s]
recalled the enchanting trill. It is not exclusively of the nestin[g]
season. A trill may be heard in winter, when the curlew [is]
down at the coast, sedately stalking across the mudflats, whe[n]
it is feeling a need to express itself between periods of probin[g]
for food.

The bill of a curlew, from which comes one of the mos[t]
stirring of wild bird calls, is a remarkable feature. There is [a]
sensitive tip. The lower third alone can be opened, which is [a]
boon when the bird is questing deeply in marshy ground. Th[e]
curlew's nostrils are set high, as though to be kept clear [of]
mud.

On Stevenson's well-remembered hills — which were i[n]
distinct contrast to the Pacific island on which he spent h[is]
last bedfast days — the curlew delivers its trill in an echo[ing]
chamber between the hill ranges. The lingering aria begin[s]
with a slow cooing sound. The speed of the crooning increase[s]
and the sound rises in pitch. The bird, having climbed steepl[y]
and hung in the air with quivering wings, is now planin[g]
towards the ground. The bubbling trill develops and end[s]
with more slow crooning.

With such a prominently vocal bird, it is a wonder tha[t]
anyone can move on the hills of early summer without seeing [a]
curlew. The curlew, a wary bird, sees all. Deer and other wil[d]
creatures must benefit from the advance warning provided b[y]
the curlew's calls of irritation. How many Jacobit[e]
sympathisers, hiding in the heather with the king's men n[ot]
far away, cursed the bird as it flew round them, shoutin[g]
lustily? Did Alan Breck, in Stevenson's *Kidnapped*, have th[e]
advantage of being pursued by Redcoats who were ignorant [of]
bird life? The pursuit was in early summer; the curlews, wit[h]
youngsters in their care, must surely have betrayed th[e]
presence of any intruder to their hills. As H.A. Gilbert wrote[,]
"When the young have hatched, no dog or human being ca[n]
moved on the hill without the whole world knowing the fact.'

Those who succeed in penetrating the bird's early warnin[g]
system may be fortunate enough to watch the mating [of]

urlews. The male makes a number of shallow depressions, in
ne of which the eggs will be laid. As it further seeks to
timulate the hen, it raises its wings upwards, trembling them
o finely they appear to shimmer, and it croons in a delightful
way.

The four eggs are large, shaped like pears. At one Highland
est I saw three eggs of normal colouration, with a ground
olour of olive-green, spotted and blotched by dark brown.
The other egg was a uniform pale greeen. Normally, the
olour of the eggs tones with the drab moorland, for not until
fter the curlews have gone does the moor go wine-red with
eather blossom.

A clutch of eggs, completed in just over a week, reclines on a
flimsy cushion of grass and is incubated for about twenty-nine
days, both parents taking a share in keeping the eggs warm.
The off-duty bird is attentive for the approach of danger. Its
trident calls are frequently heard when an arch-enemy, a
crow, is seen approaching. If eggs are taken, a repeat laying
occurs, but replacements delay the nesting programme until it
may be too late for a pair to successfully rear the young.

The curlews I saw near Loch Ness remained uneasy during
he whole time I was in the area. Even when I parked the car a
ong way from them and looked back, they were tense. I did
not see the chick again.

19

SUMMER DAYS

True summer is short-lived. It is frequently slow to develop and in a few weeks is hybridising inconspicuously with autumn. The green curtain of foliage that descended on the woods becomes shabby. A green carpet extending far up the hills soon begins to look careworn as the grasses go into decline in shades ranging from cream to brown. August holidaymakers awake to find a nip in the air. Soon there is a swirl of wizened leaves.

In the glens and by the sea is a patchwork of pastel shades where grass has been mown (frequently by hand in the case of the crofts) and the hay removed to be tucked under cover, as food for the stock in the coming winter. For a time, before the hayfields put forth spears of new growth, their hue is of palest fawn; it becomes lime green, then emerald green with the development of the second flush of grass. Hayfields untouched by artificial fertilisers are floriferous, herby. Where reseeding has taken place there is the tedium of a monoculture – one strain of grass, one overall shade of green.

The Highland summer drones with insects. Red deer, having taken themselves off to the tops, lie in the cool breezes sweeping up from the glen. Or stags plunge into peaty wallows. Both sexes occasionally immerse themselves in the water of burns. Here they can cool off and have a merciful relief from the torment of insects.

Summer is heady with scent. It permeates a languid day until a thunderstorm moves across the scene to cleanse and cool the air. When sunlight returns, the landforms glisten.

Bare hilltops never seem to catch the spirit of summer. The

tones may be baked by day, but the night will be chilly. The
ptarmigan tend their young with such devotion they thrash
the ground with their wings a few feet from a human intruder
who locates their chicks. The precocious young birds take to
the air in about ten days. One wonders how their stubby
wings have the strength to carry them.

On lower ground the young of red grouse — a species less
common in the West Highlands than it was — have a speedy
development. A grouse chick can run shortly after it has
hatched; it has enough feathering on its wings at the age of ten
days to be able to make short flights. In another ten days, the
grouse is flying reasonable distances with strength and
confidence, though it will live, perhaps find a territory, mate
and eventually die in a limited area of ground.

Also sedentary are the adult golden eagles. Summer is
benevolent to them, yet they are also stay-at-homes, flying
around the highest, loneliest crags in winter. A golden eagle,
weighing about eleven pounds, needs a considerable amount
of flesh-food to keep it healthy. It has the ability to fast for
several days in lean times — to perch for hours, just ticking
over, until more food is available. Eyries are well-spaced, each
pair ensuring there is enough food available for its needs.

Young eagles, which make their first flights in summer, and
will in due course have to find territories of their own, spend
anything up to three months at the nursery stage. The old
birds teach them the rudiments of survival, in particular how
to catch food. An adult eagle I saw by a loch near the head of a
glen had its talons clasped around the battered corpse of a
hare or rabbit.

The stalker had told me that eagles were present. When the
loch came into view a bird arose, flapping a little, then relying
on the lift provided by the breeze beneath the broad wings
which span over six feet. The golden eagle appeared from no
more than 200 yards away but soon put a considerable
distance between us. The prey, dangling from one foot,
became curiously elongated, giving the eagle a notable
silhouette. The golden eagle, hunting mainly at first light,

sometimes lifts to its eyrie the crushed corpse of a fox cub.

I came face to face with a Highland fox, but not in the wild. This fox had been reared from cubhood by a friend at a wooden-framed house near the Great Glen. Now the fox inhabited an area shaded by Scots pine. A hut was erected into which it could go for shelter and sanctuary.

My friend had ingeniously strung a wire between trees several hundred yards apart. Another wire, extending from this main wire to the collar of the fox, could be moved freely. Thus the fox had considerable scope for action. My presence excited it. For a moment or two my nostrils held the nasty flat tang of fox. When the animal bounded away, a breeze soon dispersed the cloud of fox scent.

Soon after dawn, I walked across the hills to where water had collected in a fold in the landscape. Here I watched common gulls. The name 'common' is deceptive. This gull is not as common as other gull species in the British context. The lochan was unspoilt; no-one had plugged and raised the level of its outflow to turn it into a static water tank for a village or a source of hydro-electricity. Moorland lay round about. Soon the dark mass would show the purple of the bellheather, then the regal magnificence of massed ling blossom.

The colony of common gulls was established on an islet carpeted by heather. Seeing a cloud of gulls I was reminded of a winter day by Ullswater in the Lake District, when I saw an assembly for roosting estimated to contain 13,000 common gulls.

Midsummer sees the dispersal of young gulls. At the time of my visit, birds fledging up would be crouching under the ample cover of the heather. An excited parent gave a drawling "keeah" as it circled near me.

The mewing calls of common gulls are easier to bear than the raucous din of black-headed gulls, or even the ringing outbursts of the herring gulls. Each common gull call merged into an acceptable medley when I came into sight of the lochan. Earlier, a sharp-eyed gull appeared above a ridge and

Loch Arkaig

(above) Young common g[

(left) Young curlew

Blackface ewe and lamb

A red-throated diver at its nest

Waterfall near Loch Ness

y its manner and calls alerted the others.

At another lochan, close to a busy road, common gulls esting on an island flew to the roadside as each car stopped. t was clear from their manner that they expected to be fed! Reaching the area in the early morning, I used the car as a nobile hide. When the shock waves of my intrusion had ispersed, a sandpiper tripped along the shore. A red-breasted nerganser, paddling five feet from the bank (and thus about fteen feet from the car), showed off its red bill (which is urned up at the end), a rust-brown head crested with black, nd a grey body speckled with white. The merganser flew. Bold white flashed on its wings.

Summer is a time when young peregrines, nesting on a cliff rom which they might scan a mile or two of glen, flash owards the rock, their forms looking in silhouette like rossbows. Flying high, they could see what I surveyed only fter a long slog from the floor of the glen — summering red eer, spread around the hills in areas where holidaymakers id not venture.

By late summer, red stags become assertive. A red stag oted for its pugnacity not only faced but attacked a car in a emote glen. A man was driving the car this way one October ight. He saw the stag holding its ground before him. The stag harged; £100 worth of damage was inflicted on the vehicle efore the animal gralloched itself.

Summer, alas, is for heartaches. In another glen, I saw a amily prepare to leave the Highlands for a new life in England. The removal van they hired bore a London address. ts cheery Cockney attendants, overawed at the unfamiliar ight of soaring hills, asked the usual question, "What did you nd to do in winter?"

The stalker and his family did not want to leave the glen. Their home, though old, was comfortable. They enjoyed an utdoor life uncluttered by other humans. Two pairs of golden agles nested in the area. In winter the stalker fed about sixty tags which descended the hill to the back of the house in the gloaming. Now the stalker was to take up a job where animal were in cages and paddocks. Not far away would be th sprawl of a large city.

Neighbours arrived with offers of help and sandwiches Their friendliness made the parting even harder to endure The stalker loved his work but, alas, "the money's not right" He had been lucky to clear £15 a week.

We chatted about the old days. His eyes misted up. *"Na'n b'e an diugh an d'e,"* he muttered, immediately offering translation: "Were today yesterday."

His sentiments would have struck a chord of emotion in many West Highland hearts.

INDEX